A new world awaits you...

RECREATING EARTH

Metatron's Blueprint for A Whole New World

VICTORIA REYNOLDS

Recreating Earth: Metatron's Blueprint for a Whole New World

The intent of this author is to offer information of a general nature to assist in the creation of a new reality for all life on Earth. The information provided within these pages is based on the author's personal insights.

Because of the dynamic nature of the Internet, any web addresses or links contained in this book may have changed since publication and may no longer be valid. Published by:

Freestyle Press
Hermosa Beach, CA

ISBN: 978-1-954250-09-3 (ebk)
ISBN: 978-1-954250-08-6 (sb)

Freestyle Press

Other Books by
Victoria Reynolds

Transcending Fear
Own Your True Worth
Free Your Spirit
Rise Up
Little Marigold

The Law of One

All people and all of creation are One Being:
the One Infinite Creator as unique emanations of spirit.

CONTENTS

INTRODUCTION

Who We Are   1

Earth Rising   5

Metatron and His Cube   10

THE NEW EARTH PLAN

Mission 1. End All Poverty and Hunger   21

Mission 2. Ensure Global Peace and Harmony   21

Mission 3. Ensure Excellent Health, Wellness & Wellbeing 22

Mission 4. Create Superior Education   22

Mission 5. Guaranteed Equality for All   23

Mission 6. Maintain Clean Water and Healthy Sanitation   23

Mission 7. Ensure Free Energy   24

Mission 8. End Working for Money   24

Mission 9. Build Better Infrastructure   24

Mission 10. Support International Equality   25

Mission 11. Recreate Human Settlements   25

Mission 12. Change Production Processes   26

Mission 13. Restore Climate Balance   26

Mission 14. Conserve and Restore Oceans   27

Mission 15. Protect and Restore Ecosystems   27

Mission 16. Promote Peaceful Societies   27

Mission 17. Create New Entertainment   28

Mission 18. Strengthen Mutual Support   28

THE SYSTEMS

System 1. Education   34

  Reconstruction   34

  Learning through Play   36

  New Earth Education   38

  Shifting Focus   42

  The Atmosphere   46

  Learning Center and Classroom Models   51

System 2. Healthcare   54

  Medicine and Wellness   54

  Healing Modalities   56

  Healthcare Centers   58

  Wellness Center Models   61

System 3. Environment   63

  Beyond Sustainability   63

  Human Habits   65

  Unifying   66

System 4. Agriculture   68

  Earth Domain   68

  Nature's Way   71

  Garden Models   75

System 5. Governance   77

  Self-Governance   77

  Ending Old Structures   79

  Restructuring   82

  Leadership Framework   85

  Taxation and Social Programs   89

  Governance Models   92

System 6. Economics   93

    Slave Economy   93

    Free Enterprise   95

    Heart Work   99

    Sharing as Currency   101

    Money and Banking   102

    Less is More   104

    Financial Choices   105

    Corporate Structure Model   107

System 7. Military   108

    Outgrowing Fear   108

    Choosing Love   109

System 8. Development   111

    Cityscapes   111

    Working Spaces   113

    New Communities   115

System 9. Family   119

    Family Redefined   119

    Living Environment   124

    Home Models   127

System 10. Spirituality   131

    Religion and Spirituality   131

    Spiritual Centers   133

System 11. Technology   135

    Technological Advancements   136

    Personal Experiences   137

System 12. Energy   139

Harnessing Energy 139

Powered by Nature 141

Waste-less 141

Energy Sufficient 143

Your Energy 144

System 13. Entertainment 147

Response to Fear 147

New Stories 150

Conscious Media 151

THE SOLUTIONS

Solution 1. Rethink Education 160

Solution 2. Focus on Wellbeing 164

Solution 3. Replenish the Environment 166

Solution 4. Grow Better Agriculture 168

Solution 5. Replace Governance 171

Solution 6. Create New Economics 173

Solution 7. Let Go of Defense 176

Solution 8. Consciously Develop 178

Solution 9. Expand Relationships 180

Solution 10. Grow Spiritually 182

Solution 11. Embrace Technology 184

Solution 12. Understand Energy 187

Solution 13. Enjoy Entertainment 189

RESOURCES

Adult Education and Membership 196

New Earth Projects 196

Health and Wellness 196

Domes, Homes, and Construction   196

Greenhouses and Gardens   197

Books and Reading   198

Living Off Grid   198

Metatron's Cube   199

ABOUT THE AUTHOR

INTRODUCTION

INTRODUCTION

The saying, "doing the same thing over and over again and expecting different results" has been attributed to Albert Einstein. While this was intended for scientific methods it rings true for all areas of life. Simply put, nothing changes unless something changes. I have found in watching how the human story repeats itself, the real definition of insanity is *believing* the same thing over and over again and expecting different results, because actions always stem from beliefs. Change your beliefs and your actions change with them. Change your actions and everything changes! Changing the world requires a change in personal and collective beliefs. When enough of us update our beliefs out of fear and into love, our entire reality will shift.

Who We Are

The recent rhetoric being sold to human beings is that they are the vilest existence on Earth and are incapable of change. This is one of the greatest lies ever told to humankind. Human beings only need remember who they are and rebecome who they were always meant to be. When they remember, everything on Earth will change.

Human beings are among the most extraordinary beings and creations in the known universe. Our minds are so advanced they can create with simply a thought yet so permeable they can be easily programmed by the thoughts and words of others. We have hearts so powerful they can move mountains and generate love, and so gentle they are easily broken. We have bodies that are so flexible they can be transformed and so delicate they can be prone to disease. Our limitless souls elected to learn in an environment so complex it forges spiritual mastery and generates quantum leaps of growth only experienced in human form.

Unfortunately, many have never been told of the truth of how extraordinary human beings are. They have not been taught of our true role as caretakers of Earth and our heart-to-heart connection with our collective mother. In a world propagated by fear, humanity was fed the lie that human nature is cruel, and we exist for nothing more than competition, control, conflict, and conquest of all life. This is a false narrative intended to prevent us from uniting in the truth. Humanity's true nature is caring, compassion, cooperation and cocreation. Love is the very core of the magnificent human design.

Humanity's endurance on the landscape of Earth did not come through competition and survival of the fittest, rather, it has always come through compassion and working together. Human beings are creators, designed to create and continually evolve through experience. When humanity remembers its true nature, our world will change forever, and we will create the world we have always been capable of creating and just didn't know how.

We are amid the greatest awakening and transition Earth and her beings have ever known. We stand at the brink between creating two opposing realities; unconsciously advancing the old fear-based world into global totalitarianism through digitization and transhumanism or consciously cocreating a new love-based existence through humanitarianism, unified through the spirit of compassion and Divine enlightenment. The humanitarian heart will win over the constructs of control when enough of humanity remembers how powerful we truly are. A new Earth is coming and each of us play a vital role in its creation.

If you are new to me and my work, let me begin by introducing myself. I am what some refer to as an angelic walk-in. I am Victoria, Elohim of Freedom embodied in human form. As with many of my soul family, I chose to incarnate at this time to help humanity move through this extraordinary transition between worlds and inter-create a new reality now ready to be birthed. The Elohim are creators or worlds, angelic beings who serve and assist The One Creator, Source of all that is. Many Angelic Guardians, Ascended Masters and benevolent Star Family have volunteered to take on human form at this time. They have chosen to guide humanity upward into new realms of possibility for both the human and Earth experience.

As one of these beings I telepathically communicate with others in the Angelic Realm, Guardians of Light, and with Mama Gaia as I choose to call beloved Mother Earth. Together, in what is known as The Alliance (Galactic Alliance, Alliance of Light, New Earth Alliance) we are working in harmony to lead humanity into a world that may seem impossible, yet is very, very real.

I've been asked by Mother Earth and The Guardians of Light to share the vision of what is possible for all of humanity and the role each being can each play in helping to create a new reality. This future is already written and merely needs humanity to make it manifest through thoughts, words, and deeds. In this reality, Mama Gaia (Mother Earth) and all life on her body thrive and prosper and are at peace in all things. This is a reality where our individual hearts work and beat in one with her heart and the heart of Divine Love.

We, *all* loving beings who have incarnated at this time, are the ones we've been waiting for, and we are the ones who will save humanity from the old story wanting to hold all of life captive to a world based in fear. Our consciousness and a desire for a better world is collapsing the world around us. As the old world begins crumbling beneath the weight of change, it is vital we take destiny into our own hands, rather than waiting for heroes, and begin creating the world we want to see.

The more we gather as unified minds and hearts, stepping into divinely inspired action, the sooner this magnificent new reality will manifest for all. The quicker we stop seeing each other as the enemy and unify in purpose, the sooner the old constructs will fall by the wayside. Humanity must let go of all concepts and constructs of division and see past the rhetoric created to keep us all under control. Unified, we are an unstoppable force for good.

Earth Rising

There is an old saying, "Why try to fix what isn't broken?" The truth is, it's all broken. Humanity has spent decades, centuries, and even millennia, trying to fix and bandage broken systems and structures, remodeling to the degree where no amount of gum, glue, or masking tape will hold them together. The masking tape and glue are deteriorating, exposing the remaining structures with cracks and decay, and revealing the controls attempting to hold it together.

The old world is crumbling and all its systems with it. Rather than trying to fix all the broken systems and hold them together with more fear and control, it is time for humanity to simply replace what isn't working and start entirely new. It is time to construct a new world, keeping in mind the lessons learned from the past and seeing what doesn't work.

Out of the ashes of an old, dying world, a new Earth is rising. The old world isn't the planet herself, but a world of concepts and systems which are no longer viable and no do not serve the highest and greatest good of all. Earth is being restored to her fullest potential along with the beings which inhabit her body. We are returning to Gaia's Garden, a place of peace and respite for the souls who choose to live here.

All third dimension, lower vibrational, fear-based systems and existing structures have begun failing and will collapse under the weight of many truths being revealed as deception loses its cover. The veil between realities is being torn away and dissolved, never to be used again. Light is exposing the darkness and learning through the contrast is coming to an end. Collectively, humanity will begin moving into a fifth dimensional, love-based reality. Together we are bringing heaven to Earth though our inner resonance and choices.

These dimensions are dimensions of consciousness rather than physical dimensions. For many thousands of years, Earth and humanity have been experiencing a third-dimensional reality where fear is prevalent in all things and provides a contrast for learning. Fear offers an excellent medium for growth and aligns with darkness. New life is seeded in darkness before emerging into light and part of the human challenge is for each of us to find our light within the darkness and remember love within the fear. Moving from this dense third dimension and into the fifth dimension of consciousness requires letting go of all that remains of the third dimension and its fear-based concepts.

The fourth dimension is a necessary part of the process, allowing humanity to move easily between worlds and let go of all lower dimensional beliefs and constructs. The convergence of the fourth dimension of consciousness with the third dimension in 2012 made it possible for humanity to begin seeing the duality in our reality and consciously choose love over fear. This convergence made it possible for many to begin seeing beyond the veil of deception and activate spiritual gifts they were previously unaware of. Those who choose love feel drawn to a fifth dimension of consciousness, a fifth density, where there is only love exists and love governs all things. This reality based on love is what many have foretold as New Earth and Heaven on Earth.

The fourth-dimension bridge, also recognized as a spiritual spiral upward, is the space where humanity faces the great challenge of letting go. Humanity is being asked to let go of everything that no longer serves what is best for our individual and collective reality and release it all back into the hands of creation. As we let go and detach from past expectations, we grow in our enlightenment and experience the beginning stages of recreating our individual and collective reality.

We face the greatest time of change the Earth has ever known, at least in the time known to humankind. This is a time that has been foretold by many, for many thousands of years. We are recreating Earth and the entire human experience. The New Earth has already been created in the etheric realm and each of us is a part in making it manifest into physical reality. Each being plays a role in recreating every aspect of the human experience. Every system will be rethought entirely through a new unified mind and heart.

For this New Earth plan to be fully consummated and thrive, it is vital all human beings move out of any form of competition and division and replace all previous concepts with collaboration, cooperation, and unification. This is the only way humanity will survive and thrive as together we move beyond the crumbling infrastructures of the past. Civilizations have come and gone. Civilization as we presently understand it, is ending, and a new civilization is emerging – a global civilization driven by the heart of compassion and unity of mind. As many of our societies, structures, and systems begin collapsing, they will be replaced with better, more beautiful, balanced, and harmonious structures in service to the whole.

This recreation of our world will require those of us with vision and foresight to begin the process of establishing these new structures and concepts as we work together to build the foundation for our new world. Every aspect of our reality is shifting and will be replaced with all things new. Nothing will be left untouched as we see the potential in all things and work to redefine them with new understanding.

This emergence and rising has already begun behind closed doors, in quiet communities and social settings. Rumblings of new ideas are bubbling to the surface for all to see. Small ideas become vast visions which will transform landscapes. Once new concepts are proven on individual and community scales, they will spread outward across cities, states, countries, and the Earth, creating an entirely new way of living and being, not seen since Earth was a garden of peace.

The present transition phase for humanity will not be easy. Many will continue clinging to old stories, long-held beliefs, and ways of moving through life. They will look longingly at the past and hold on to what is comfortable and known. There is no going back. For some, their gentle hearts will be unable to process the change and their souls will choose to opt-out of the ascension process as Earth and her beings rise into higher awareness and a new age of enlightenment. Other souls who cannot raise their resonance from fear to love will also be leaving the playing field. Understand my loves, it is simply a soul's choice whether to weather the storm or leave the Earth realm. Simply love them forward as their souls venture elsewhere.

Metatron and His Cube

The content in this book is communicated to me from Archangel Metatron, supported by the heart of Gaia to the hearts of her children, and by the Mother/Father Creator along with Yeshua, master teacher for planet Earth. As the Scribe of God and keeper of the Akashic Records, Archangel Metatron holds and maintains the records for all that was, all that is, and all that will be. Through my interpretation he teaches us about the future for our planet and gives us clues on how best to use his Cube as a blueprint for creation. He shares an overview of the future of humanity and all life on Earth and the world we will create once enough of us decide to choose it and do the work necessary to create it.

For those who are committed to the betterment of humanity and creation of our new world, it is time to start thinking outside all boxes, and rather, begin thinking within the cube – Metatron's Cube. While the concept of a cube has been used by some as a container for restricting life, Metatron's Cube holds infinite possibilities. Within its design are all the building blocks, forms, and geometric designs for creating entirely new realities. These designs are often referred to as sacred geometry.

Metatron's Cube is used as a model for new concepts to replace existing systems and controls on the planet. It creates balance in all things with no one at the helm and everyone working in cooperation for the best of all living kind. The models provided within herein are not the only way to recreate human concepts, however, they do offer a guide and framework for envisioning what is possible. They are provided to stimulate your creative vision and open your minds to new potentialities. When sacred geometry is used with intentional creation, humanity will astound itself with what is possible.

At the center is this multi-faceted and multi-purposeful design, there is the cube for which this all-encompassing sacred geometry is named. This multi-dimensional cube holds within it the library for creation and allows for plot points within a given time and space field for movement between realities. It's easier to navigate the concept of time and space if it is plotted within a container.

Metatron's Cube is the label given to this sacred multi-dimensional geometric shape which extends beyond our present elements of understanding. It contains within it, all geometric shapes, and patterns, offering limitless possibilities for creation and acts as a web for holding relationships, businesses, systems, organizations, and all of life together in balance and harmony and in the natural resonance and rhythms of creation.

Every operation on Earth, when patterned within the forms found in this geometric design, becomes a cohesive part of the whole, binding all aspects of the human experience into Oneness in mind, body, heart, and spirit. Its energetic imprint opens up a world of possibilities through interconnectedness in all things. Through it, the illusion of separation disappears, and all beings are fully empowered as light beings having a human experience. The energy emitted through The Cube empowers human potential.

Metatron's Cube gives humanity a new approach to all of our structures, concepts, and systems. Looking at it from a multi-dimensional perspective, we can see even more what it has to offer as we reconstruct our world. It is more than simply a design for hanging on walls for decoration or for energizing our personal spaces, it offers the understanding of how energy moves between form and how we can use those forms and lay lines for creating our projects, structures, systems and services.

The primary content in this book focuses on using circles, circularity, and the Law of Circulation for making our world a better place. The circles found within Metatron's Cube represent the feminine aspects of creation. The hard angles, which create squares and triangles are a representation of the masculine. In this new reality, we are balancing both the masculine and feminine to work in harmony and cooperation for the greatest good of all. As we balance both the masculine and feminine across all conceivable concepts, all beings are lifted up and supported and all life on Earth wins.

Why This Book?

Many of my readers and viewers have asked me where to start in the creation of New Earth. There are now hundreds of millions of people across the Earth realm who are choosing to actively participate in creating a new reality based on love, and simply need guidance about what to envision, how to start, and where to participate.

This book offers solutions to Earth's present problems and a blueprint for creating New Earth to serve the highest and greatest good of all concerned, in the truth that all are one. As humanity evolves to self-regulate through love, all known systems will eventually dissolve away. The game of contrast, of light and dark, is coming to an end. The collective of souls have chosen to no longer learn through the contrast, and role of Earth as a learning planet is fading away as we transition to a planet of peace.

It is now time for those working in the light to become just as organized and strategic as the dark side has always been. It is time to let go of all terms and constructs intended to divide us and prevent us from experiencing the full power of unity. It is time to unify under the banner of love. As humanity unifies in mind, heart, and spirit, all things become possible, and all life on Earth is forever changed. The time of, "What's in it for me?", is over as together we embrace, "What's best for all concerned?"

I've structured the book content and the New Earth Plan as a rebuttal to the New World Agenda, using the same systems with a focus on freedom rather than control. The New World Order Agenda and New Earth Consciousness Plan may look similar on the surface but lead to two vastly different outcomes. This book offers the reader a vision beyond the present narrative into what is truly possible for humanity when "we the people" come together with "we're the ones we've been waiting for" and create a new world which works for all of us.

Along with the written concepts shared here, I am including a variety of images and diagrams to help stimulate your imagination and understanding of how you can use Metatron's Cube in your physical structures. I've also included a list of resources you may find helpful as you feel guided.

Throughout the book you may find suggestions coming from "we" rather than me as a singular author, and references to "your" and "you" which refers to us as the collective you. The content is co-written with Gaia, Metatron, Yeshua, and Source Creator as one voice through me, as it comes to me from the future already created on our behalf. The content is love-steamed through me from higher realms and refers to us on Earth as "you" and "yours." You will also find diagrams throughout at the end of some chapters to help you envision the concepts presented here. Those patterned after Metatron's Cube are designed through me and with my limited graphic design capabilities. The others are images courtesy of multiple resources listed in the resources section in the final chapter.

THE
PLAN

Section 1
THE NEW EARTH PLAN

There is a new mission for Planet Earth. That overarching mission is to create a planet which is paradise rather than the learning planet it has been in the past. The time of Earth as a school for souls is complete and now comes the time of peace and plentitude.

The plan for 2030 and beyond ensures peace, prosperity, health, freedom, and happiness for all life on Earth. You, the people and beings of Earth, have entered the transition phase between realities and here you will lay the groundwork for New Earth. The primary focus for now and moving forward, until humanity reaches the following phase of Absolute Oneness, will be on clean up and restoration. As your old systems crumble and fall, all focus will go toward cleaning up the mess made by those in fear and creating new concepts serving all life on Earth. Even the concept of systems will be replaced by more liberating concepts based on individuality, harmony, and unity rather than systemization.

All of those who choose to participate in the conscious evolution of humanity will be working together in creating Earth from the ground up. You will be rethinking every concept and setting missions and plans in place to harmonize, support and thrive, making choices only from a heart of mutual support and infinite compassion for all. As new humans who are fully restored to your capacity, you will only see and know each other through the eyes of love.

New Science will shift focus from supporting agendas back to the curiosity upon which science founded. This return to curiosity, awe, and wonder will expand the human experience into places humanity has only imagined. Humanity is continually evolving and revolutionizing itself. You are entering a new Ingenuity Revolution. This new turn will make an impact the size of your Industrial Revolutions yet without any negative impacts. Your greatest collective genius is your ability to create what you imagine. This is where the human mind shines in its brilliance. You will work together to create a new world. Once you have learned how to recreate your collective home and live in harmony with each other, Earthlings will take to the stars.

Mission 1. End All Poverty and Hunger

Through humanitarian projects and earnest goodwill, fresh, clean, plentiful water, better growing conditions for food, and opportunities for personal growth and development will be made available to those in the most impoverished places on Earth. This allows for complete self-sufficiency while also choosing what is best for their unique cultures. For those in more technologically advanced areas, humanitarian projects will teach them how to elevate themselves out of poverty and hunger to become self-sufficient and self-empowered. All programs will focus on lifting the people from within themselves, and integrating programs that work on their behalf, rather than simply taking care of them. Those who are unable to physically contribute, due to age or illness, will be honored and supported for who they are, and their non-physical gifts, rather than what they can physically contribute.

Mission 2. Ensure Global Peace and Harmony

All beliefs, rituals, and practices promoting the harm of any human or animal will be ended. All who have propagated such suffering will be removed from society either to be rehabilitated through love and understanding or separated out where they can no longer cause harm. The intentional suffering of any life, for any reason, will no longer be a concern. No being will need to be sacrificed for the wellbeing of another. There will only be infinite compassion for all beings everywhere.

Mission 3. Ensure Excellent Health, Wellness & Wellbeing

The focus of all wellbeing will be on the whole being; mind, body, heart, and spirit. All disease will be eradicated, and emphasis will be placed on ensuring the wellbeing of all beings. Technologies will be created for maximum healing and restoration of the physical body, with energetic healing modalities for the mind, heart, and spirit. The manipulation of Earth's goodness to create chemicals for modifying food will end. Food will come directly from the source and grow to its fullest potential with advanced growing techniques and will restore nature rather than depleting it.

Mission 4. Create Superior Education

Education will shift to a focus on each child's natural gifts and propensities. Systemized education of children will be replaced by individual child-centered learning models, free of agendas, promotions, affiliations, and special interests, and in learning environments which nurture kindness, mutual support, open-mindedness, genuine thoughtful communication and heartfelt understanding.

Mission 5. Guaranteed Equality for All

All human beings will be treated with equality, honor, dignity, and respect, regardless of the shade of their skin, system of belief, marital status, gender definition, year they were born, place of birth, education level or any of the labels once used to divide and belittle humanity. All beings will come to accept themselves and each other for who they are rather than societal expectations. As all labels fade away, all beings will come to see each other only as "we," unified in heart.

Mission 6. Maintain Clean Water and Healthy Sanitation

Water throughout the world will be fresh, clean, and clear of all chemicals and imbalances. It will be easily accessible for all, regardless of location and apparent limitation, and will flow freely without constraint or controls. Sanitation and cleanliness will be at the forefront, eliminating all disease and refuse. Innovations in sanitation will ensure a clean and safe environment for beings.

Mission 7. Ensure Free Energy

Existing energy systems and products will be replaced with free, clean, natural energy, easily available to all. New modalities for delivering energy will come to the forefront which cause no harm any environment. There will no longer be a desire for anyone to limit or control the energy of anyone else. All is freely given and freely received.

Mission 8. End Working for Money

All people will be encouraged to follow their heart's desires, doing work they love and in mutual support for themselves and others. All people will have their needs met and the desire for bigger and better than anyone else will be replaced with personal preference. All work will be seen as a loving service toward the betterment of humanity and the best for all concerned. While money will still exist as a means of exchange, until it is replaced by a better energetic exchange, it will no longer be the drive behind every person's existence. Creating a meaningful world will take preference over any desire for gain.

Mission 9. Build Better Infrastructure

Innovating individuals and pioneering teams will create new working and living environments that are harmonious with nature and the natural rhythms of human and universal energy. Innovations will clean and remove harsh remnants of the past, and create a lighter and brighter world, without any negative impact on the planet or all life on Earth.

Mission 10. Support International Equality

All nations and all people will be celebrated for their uniqueness and diversity and brought into sovereignty. All nations will thrive through economic equality with all other nations and generously share in the abundance of Earth's goodness. Nations will no longer be at war with their own people or each other. Instead, there will be a sense of oneness. Eventually, in one Earth consciousness, all hard borders will disappear as there will no longer be a need for national self-preservation.

Mission 11. Recreate Human Settlements

High-rise buildings with people stacked on top of each other in boxes will become a thing of the past, except for those who choose multi-layered living. An emphasis will be placed on creating new harmonious communities in concert with nature. Every home and building structure will be self-sustaining with free energy, on-site gardens, and a focus on well-being. Tall structures built by men's egos to enslave employees will be brought down and replaced by community gardens. There will be no need for security as there will be no desire to cause harm to each other. The focus of all structures will be placed on beauty and organic functionality, over how much money the building or structure can produce.

Mission 12. Change Production Processes

Production will shift from the drive for consumerism to conscious use and utilization. The supply chain will be reduced to become a "direct to customer" approach and "buy local" to ensure communities are self-sufficient while also receiving goods and services in a quick and easy fashion. There will be less of a desire for needless things and more of a desire to mutually support each other's needs. Greed and the desire for endless consumption will become a thing of the past.

Mission 13. Restore Climate Balance

Those corporations which have decimated Earth's landscape and will no longer remain. Humanitarian projects will cleanup and re-seed the planet, restoring her to her full potential to nurture and support all life. Advanced technologies will be used to rebalance the atmosphere and restore full life-giving and supporting potential across all environments.

Mission 14. Conserve and Restore Oceans

Through global humanitarian projects, the initial focus will be on ocean cleanup. Once oceans are cleaned, water life-forms will be fully rebalanced and reseeded. All oil extraction from the seabed will be terminated along with other practices which harm the delicate balance of sea life.

Mission 15. Protect and Restore Ecosystems

The focus will shift from sustainability to regeneration. All of Earth's ecosystems will be fully restored. Human technologies will work in harmony with nature through new practices which continually replenish the Earth. All ecosystems will be seen as vital, sacred, and worthy of preservation and expansion. All animals on the edge of extinction will be returned to thriving and animals will no longer be hunted for sport or profit.

Mission 16. Promote Peaceful Societies

Incarceration will shift from putting people away and punishment to learning, understanding and true rehabilitation.

This shift in consciousness will spread from ground level into every society on Earth. As all human needs are met, there will no longer be a desire for any culture or people to dominate another, take from each other, or harm each other. The focus will shift from having more to helping more.

Mission 17. Create New Entertainment

All fear-based narratives and violence in entertainment will cease to be created except when used for telling stories of the past. It will not be projected forward as a means of storytelling. Although conflict and resolution may be used as a form of showing transformation, violence will be replaced by issue resolution, thus redefining the problem/solution scenario. New entertainment will focus on possibilities and inspiration, telling new stories of how things used to be and what you are all able to create. Human beings crave inspiration and that is what they will be fed.

Mission 18. Strengthen Mutual Support

Across every city, state, country, and culture, humanity will focus on solutions rather than problems, and through co-operation will create long-lasting solutions for the betterment of all life on Earth. All concepts, systems and governances will work toward the common mission of creating a better world which works for and uplifts all living things.

The Systems

SECTION 2
THE SYSTEMS

Every system on Earth will be dissolved from their present structures and restructured as concepts which serve each community and beyond, rather than constructed as systems of control. The old concept of systems, that is systems which exist for the sole purpose of propagating and growing the system and holding humanity within systemized boxes, will cease to exist.

In the past, as humanity evolved in understanding of processes and systems, your systems became more systemized and overtook personal sovereignty. Human beings lost their autonomy and in essence became servants of the systems, rather than the systems serving the people. That time is coming to an end as all systems collapse under the weight of their top-heaviness.

As eyes are opened to how the systems have failed the people and have only served the pocketbooks of those who created the systems, human beings will gather in unity to create new concepts which serve the masses rather than the few. All systems will be reconstructed with freedom at the core. All systems will be replaced with real and genuine services. Those systems which cannot be reconstructed under love, harmony, and freedom for all, will collapse and vanish as have other systems from times gone by.

System 1. Education

The new model of education will require an entire rethinking of the existing systems which currently support a closed system over the limitless child. It is less about the welfare of the child and more about sustaining the system. When the focus shifts from, "How can we make the system work?" to "How can we help each child thrive?" everything will change.

Reconstruction

Education will be reconstructed from the ground up. Nowhere is reconstruction more important than teaching the youngest generation. What they learn will define the future of humanity. It is vital they learn in a way that has never been taught before. The human capacity is limitless and children who are not limited by dogmatic teaching will thrive in a world of endless possibilities.

Your education procedures and systems were created during the industrial revolution phase of your collective human experience. Formal education was created to keep children busy while their parents left the fields and self-sustenance to trade their time for money. Prior to that time, education was a means of teaching children the basic concepts they would need to be self-sufficient in a pre-industrial world.

As education systems across your world evolved, they became a way of indoctrinating children with concepts backed by political ideologies, just as religion indoctrinates children with religious ideologies. The younger a mind is indoctrinated the more the content is cemented and solidified. Children lose their capacity for questioning what they are learning, and their free, creative spirits become squelched.

You are now entering a new phase for humanity, and many are seeing how the archaic system of training through indoctrination does not work and is stifling to the human spirit. The child's spirit needs to be free to explore and create. You are creator beings. It is the very essence of your human blueprint. This is how you are made in the image of Prime Creator. As you rethink education, all future learning models will be based on this one primary understanding.

Learning through Play

All sentient beings learn best through play. Human beings, regardless of age, are not meant to learn through suffering but rather through joy. They are meant to learn most from doing what they love and feeling the thrill of doing it well. And yet, your present systems all appear to reinforce learning through failure and suffering of the mind, rather than through play of the heart. Your education systems were created to teach through mind memorization and programming, while ignoring the hearts of children.

Every human being is born with gifts so grand; they have within them all they need to live a joy-filled and deeply meaningful life. Those gifts have been ignored for the sake of the systems intended for social control. Your education systems, in essence, are little more than indoctrination systems and a way to keep children busy while their parents work to make money for the systems of greed. None of this is based in genuine love.

The present systems exist to serve the systems themselves, rather than serve the wellbeing of everyone. That, Dear Ones, is coming to an end. Children need to remember what it is to play and learn from the joy of their hearts. And as such, the current education systems will be replaced with educational programs which teach children how to thrive in their true giftedness.

Education will no longer be about convenience to the system, but rather will focus on the wellbeing of children, with each child celebrated for their unique gifts, talents, personalities, and propensities. When children are celebrated for who they are, competition, lack, and feelings of inadequacy disappear. This of course requires a complete re-training of the adult mind to teach in a way that serves the child and future generations, rather than serves the systems which control what teachers are allowed to teach.

At the surface, this reeducation of educators may sound difficult, and yet, so many of your teachers, for the love of children, chose to be teachers and desire to teach from their hearts of love, rather than to the restrictions imposed upon them by the system. Their hearts yearn to teach the child, through their hearts, rather than what they are told to teach. An entirely new type of teacher, one who teaches from his or her own creativity, will evolve from the education remodeling.

Children were not meant to stand in line as trained soldiers and repeat memorized sentences with no meaning to them. They are not meant to memorize facts and figures they will never use, simply for passing tests. Tests signify nothing other than to determine if a child is worthy to be recognized for their intellectual prowess in a system that only recognizes one form of intelligence and disregards the rest. Testing is simply a way of segregating some children and disregarding the rest as less-than. It is a way of searching for the cream of the crop, while assuming the rest will become worker bees. Children in this system are not brought up in their own brilliance, they are brought up to serve the systems.

New Earth Education

What then does the New Earth education look like? It celebrates the individual and the unique gifts each child brings into the world. It recognizes there are no one-size-fits-all educational programs, and every child has brilliance within them. This brilliance can take on many forms, some which have yet to be recognized by humanity because these intelligences were discounted and shamed. There is no shame in any of it. Every child is worthy of celebration and attention. Every child is gifted in their own way, and all have genius within them.

The role of the New Earth Education is to draw out each child's giftedness and expand upon it. Rather than focusing on making the system and organization work as a self-sustaining organism, all focus is shifted on what is best for children. The new models and systems work on behalf of the child rather than the system itself. The entire educational concept, from bottom to top, is to nurture and grow the unique gifts of each child. No longer will education be system-centered, teacher-centered, or parent-centered. All education will be centered around the individual needs and propensities of the child.

It is also vital to understand that child-centered doesn't mean it becomes a free-for-all and children run wild without boundaries, or where the child makes the rules and demands all adults serve him or her. It is simply to understand that education is intended to nurture and cultivate each child's natural born capacity making it possible for each to grow into fulfilled and confident adults.

Children need loving guidance, direction, and discipline, not punishment. They need supportive guidelines to feel what it means to never truly fail while learning through experience. They need to learn how to embrace opportunities for growth even in less than pleasant situations. They also need to recognize other's boundaries and learn how to set boundaries for themselves. Children don't require boxes, labels, fences, chains or guards. The boundaries they need are examples of emotional boundaries while being free to create and be themselves.

Teachers will learn to recognize how a child learns best and what a child gravitates toward. Parents who have taken the time to learn from their child, will see their gifts begin to emerge in toddlerhood. Few parents until now have taken the time or have the consciousness to recognize what delights their child and their child's innate personality, rather they insist their child becomes who the parents and the system want the child to be. The child's natural gifts are discarded by the needs of parents and educators for the child to fit into the box of who they "should" be. That mindset will disappear as the classroom is structured for expression and exploration. For example, mathematics can become play for each child when concepts are presented in a way their unique minds compute. Beyond the basics needed for everyday utility, math is only necessary for those students who love it and gravitate to the puzzle solving mathematics brings with it.

While it is vital to expose children to many forms of learning, and potential skills, forcing them to learn what doesn't resonate with them only stifles their full potential and lessens their confidence. Children who learn through their natural propensity and follow a learning path which best suits them, thrive. In this truth, the concept of teaching for a passing grade becomes obsolete as children will be graded on their natural progression of understanding rather than for the sake of test passing. Schools will no longer be rewarded for the grades of their students but be celebrated for how well children thrive in their learning environment.

In the New Earth, all schooling is hands-on. Children learn best through experiencing the learning rather than being told what to think. There will be no more learning to test, rather, there will questioning to see if the learning integrated. Children will be taught how to question everything without fear or doubt and to trust their own inner guidance. They will learn through active cooperation rather than through programming. Students who have integrated the learning will assist the teacher by working with other students who require more explanation, thereby helping both students learn through caring interaction which further integrates the learning. Students will learn self-trust through conscious choices and build inner confidence through apparent failure with sincere encouragement.

Educators and counsellors will need to be reeducated in interpersonal studies of compassionate communication, mutual understanding, and conscious discipline through love, rather than punishment through fear. Teachers will also learn life-lesson and issue resolution, heart-centered leadership, and active listening. Rather than chastising students for their apparent failures and mistakes, students will learn hands-on conscious-issue resolution through mutual support and understanding. They will learn to listen to themselves through mindfulness and inner focus, and genuinely care about how their choices affect others.

School counselors will have an extended background and understanding of spiritual psychology and loving mediumship, allowing them to understand their students on a deep inner level and see into their being. In essence the school psychologist is also psychic, with ability to see within and beyond the student's present circumstances and feel into a child's needs.

Children will be allowed to feel love and compassion from those who are nurturing them on their path. As all manner of fear and what you call evil is swept from the Earth, children will become free to be children. They will go to the bathroom without the need for a bathroom buddy, hug their teachers, caregivers, and volunteers, and yes, even talk to strangers. There will be no reason for doubt or mistrust of anyone.

Shifting Focus

The focus on learning throughout the entire educational program will shift from memorizing facts and figures to learning usable skills. Questioning and learning multiple perspectives will be encouraged for mutual support and understanding. In older classrooms, students will no longer be required to have textbooks and lectures which do not stimulate the mind. This is a waste of mind space. Rather, the teacher may play a movie, then lead the classroom in an open discussion about the movie to extrapolate the many learning opportunities and opinions about the information contained within the movie. This is one example of learning through entertainment.

Reading will remain a vital part of learning as reading exercises and develops the mind, however, students will have more options to read material they gravitate toward, rather than books designated by the system with specific agenda. Focus will be placed on the student's confidence to present their material rather than the subject of the material. Each child's confidence becomes evident when they do work they enjoy, and present work they enjoyed preparing. Some children will prefer written presentations. Others may prefer verbal. And there may be others who choose a graphic approach. All are encouraged equally.

Schools will be based in a cooperative model where every parent equally contributes time, money, and energy into the education of their children. Lower grade levels will offer learning tracks for students who have begun to show a propensity toward a particular focus of learning. For example, some students who show signs of a preference for art, will take a creative tract for all their learning, and expand on their creative propensities. Students who show a preference for math will take a math tract to further expand their understanding and so on. No one tract is considered more valuable than another as they are all equally valued and supported.

There will also be schools which focus on a particular tract, for example, you may create schools for older children, which focus only on creativity, science, mathematics, language, or physical skills. There will be a return to apprenticeship and community involvement allowing for every child to learn through hands-on experience. All education leads to a focus on free enterprise, community impact, the betterment of humanity, and loving your work, rather than working for money.

Every school will have an on-site garden where students will participate in the growing process from planting, weeding, nurturing, harvesting, and composting, to understanding and appreciating the web of life and all ecosystems. Food grown in the garden will be used in the school kitchen and children are invited to be a part of the food preparation process. This is one example of hands-on science while also learning invaluable life skills. Daily classes also include meditation, mindfulness, and exercise with a focus on whole-self wellbeing. Every drop of time spent in the learning environment will be toward the betterment of the child's life experience.

New Earth schools are all cooperative and community-based, free of all indoctrination, propaganda, and agenda. There will be quiet time set aside throughout the day for reflection, spiritual practice, or meditation, for children to use in a way that best serves them. Mutual understanding and support will be at the core of the entire educational experience. All opinions and beliefs are considered and reflected upon. All children are created equal, all are loved, and all are worthy of respect.

The focus of education models will be determined by individual communities and those within each community. Some communities may prefer larger education centers similar to existing schools, while others will prefer a more relaxed and intimate atmosphere. This will be a matter of community and personal choice, rather than a choice made by a public system. As private, community-based schools, teachers are not required to follow state and federal mandates and are free to teach from their hearts. Parents are encouraged to be a part of the education process, from volunteering on the playground and helping the teacher, to leading in the classroom setting. This is particularly to older classrooms as parents volunteer to teach their own set of skills while opening children's minds to limitless possibilities for themselves. All education programs are focused on teaching life skills and expanded awareness of the world around them rather than focused on generic information.

The Atmosphere

The physical structure of each classroom and the school buildings themselves may best be served as dome-shaped classrooms and open rotundas rather than the present boxes used to corral children into their rows and cubicles. Open-dome structures provide for better acoustics and energy flow. When considering the restructuring of your education programs, thinking outside the box regarding physicality of structures will prove to be an improvement over all previous concepts and designs.

The New Earth classroom looks very different from classrooms of the past. Classrooms will allow for as much fresh air and interaction with nature as possible. Classrooms with sliding glass panels which open to nature will create a terrarium approach to education while also providing shelter from the elements when needed. Fresh air, sunshine, and personal creativity will take precedence over controlled curriculum. Students will use the outdoors as a classroom, and experience free play, as much as possible. Play is necessary for the mind to integrate what it has learned. Puppies, kittens, and other animals will be an important part of each classroom environment, helping children with compassion, mutual care, responsibility, and play. Children of all ages will learn the value of life and the love of beings other than human.

This new way of learning and teaching is not a return to the one-room classroom with a schoolmarm but a classroom where all students learn the value of cooperation and mutual respect. Parents are encouraged at all grade levels to participate both in the classroom and on the playground, not for the sake of their own children, but for the wellbeing of all children. Loving parental participation breeds children's self-confidence and builds trusting relationships with adults.

In circular schools there are learning interactive circles and circle tables, rather than rows of obedient students. Each table hosts a learning environment which best serves the learning style of the student. Each circle focuses on learning in a unique way and the children in the learning circle are supported by a hands-on teacher, rather than a lecturer.

For example, mathematics may work best in one learning circle where the students thrive who are more visual and excel with the more traditional learning method. Another learning circle where children are more tactile will require a more physical approach to math and a touching method. Another learning table where the children may have an inclination toward art will allow students to draw out math through art forms. Some children who are more auditory may need to talk the concepts through.

The teacher sits in the center and uses a wheeled chair to easily navigate around the center circle to support students sitting at each of the circle tables. These learning pods help everyone thrive in their chosen environment. Education won't be about doing it the right way, but in a way which encourages the concepts to stick without a child feeling judged for learning differently from others.

At higher levels of education, schools specializing in a variety of interests and skill development will replace schools in which every child is educated with the same information, regardless of their gifts and propensities. Some children may choose a math track and others may choose an art track or a skill for a trade track, leading to higher education catering to the child's interests and propensities rather than forcing them to learn redundant information.

As the world expands in awareness, advanced education, for those who choose to continue an educational track, may include such subjects as Earth Restoration, Source Code, Light Language, Creation Geometry, Quantum Studies, Intergalactic Relations, Telepathic and Psychic Development, Spiritual Psychology, Conscious Communication, Universal Law, and Whole-Body Healing along with a host of other courses which have yet to be explored by the human mind. Education will focus on creating a better and cooperative world, rather than education for the sake of education.

Every student graduating from the education programs will have usable life skills they can utilize to support themselves, their families, and their communities. Post-high school education will no longer be pushed as a social requirement and will rather be a choice for those who desire to continue learning. Every person will be valued for who they are and their unique contribution to society rather than how much schooling they have and their level of educational intelligence.

College degrees will no longer be used as a filter for getting a job, as jobs working for someone else simply for a paycheck and benefits will become a thing of the past. Those who choose to be employed will be employed based on their skills and inclinations, rather than an expensive degree or where they went to school. Colleges will focus on expanding students' skills and interests, rather than learning for the sole purpose of a diploma and its accolades. In this understanding, all children will thrive in a world of their own making, rather than a world crafted by others, allowing only some to thrive.

This new way of educating begins with parents and teachers having a willingness to pull themselves out of the existing system and create their own private and cooperative educational programs. It requires the ability to see with an open mind of possibilities, rather than relying on systems of control. Yes, all change requires a willingness to take risks. Nothing will change until human beings are willing to step into the unknown, elicit change, and lead the way for others to follow.

Eventually, there will no longer be an education "system," as this, along with all other systems are dismantled. The education systems will be replaced with community-led education models, allowing parents, educators, and communities to choose the models that best serve the needs of the younglings in their care.

Learning Center and Classroom Models

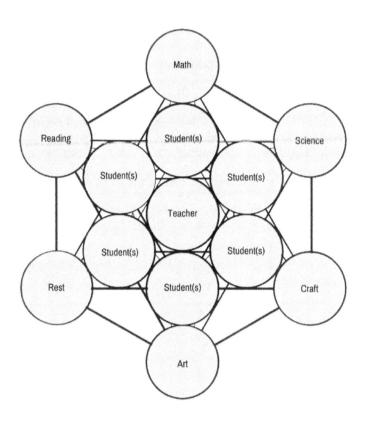

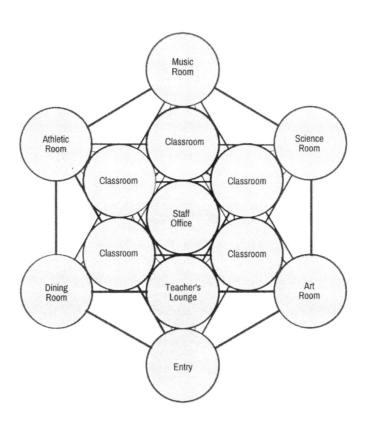

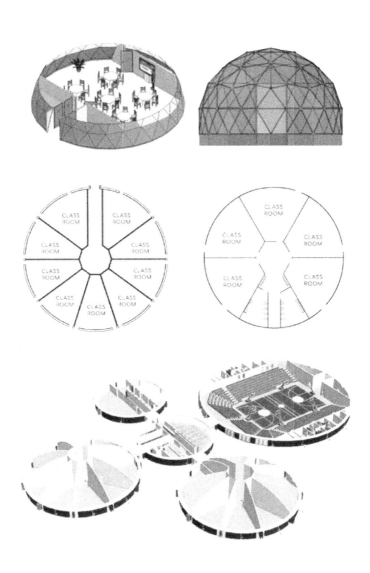

System 2. Healthcare

The Divine Human is one of the finest creations in all the Universe. You have minds so effective you can create with your thoughts. Your hearts are so powerful they are generators of love. Your bodies are so strong you can build anything you imagine. Your spirits are so limitless you are driven by freedom. You are now only beginning to understand your true nature and multi-dimensional capabilities

Medicine and Wellness

As you move forward you will begin to astound yourselves with what is possible once you free your minds from the present limitations and controls. Over the recent centuries, healthcare has devolved from wellness and a mastery of healing arts to practicing with a continually changing flow of information, chemistry and profitability and moving from focusing on wellness to focusing on sickness.

Your present day medical systems exist to promote chemicals rather than real healing. This artificial healing centers on symptoms rather than prevention, cause, and cure. While the mind/body relationship is now more formally understood, and the physical makeup of the body more known, the inner workings of cause and effect have been largely ignored because illness is more profitable than wellness. Each of your body systems and functions all work in tandem and harmony with each other. When this is out of balance it affects the rest. This has yet to be fully explored in your world of wellbeing. You are only now just beginning to understand how the mind, heart, body and soul work together as one unit.

As you recreate your present medical systems, the purpose of all healthcare will shift from sickness to wellness of the whole being. It will shift to prevention of illness and all disease, rather than your present model of medicating and artificial treatment for the purpose of greed. There will be a return to caring for the human vessel for the pure love of caring.

The human avatar is an extraordinary creation, able to remedy and restore itself when given the proper environment for wholeness. When the mind, body, heart, soul are well, all aspects of life mirror that wellness. Personal well-being will be at the forefront of all human choices. As you shift your focus from sickness to wellness, every choice you make will take your mental, emotional, physical and spiritual wellness into consideration.

Ease is the natural state of being for all beings. Anything that is not a constant state of ease becomes disease. The focus will be on maintaining a state of ease for the whole being. This new focus will allow for the human body to be restored to its fullest divine human potential and continual ease, maintained through self-care. Maintaining a state of ease will begin before birth and continue throughout an entire lifetime.

Healing Modalities

The focus will shift to wellness rather than sickness and on prevention before treatment. All treatments will work toward curing the cause of illness when it occurs, rather than treating symptoms. Treating the whole being concentrates on the initial cause of illness: mentally, emotionally, physically, and spiritually, and treats the cause, thus eliminating symptoms.

Medical personnel will be trained in cures and preventions provided by Earth's goodness and advanced healing technologies rather than defaulting to chemical compounds backed by greed. Better living through chemistry as some now see it, will become an archaic approach to healthcare. The chemical industry, which includes pharmaceuticals, will no longer participate in every aspect of Earth's existence. It will be disinvited from the game, other than to create honest solutions for all life on Earth. Chemicals will no longer poison air, water, land, or beings, directly contributing to more illness and disguised as medicine. Chemical influence will be replaced by genuine healing and curing all disease on both the body of the planet and the bodies of all her beings.

Physicians will learn advanced healing modalities in "new medicine" and will focus on healing, while medicating as a last resort rather than as a first response. Healthcare professionals will no longer "practice" medicine, rather, they will become healers of the human mind, body, heart, and spirit gifted at knowing how to help the whole being heal itself.

New technology will be created whereby the body can be cured of all injury, and all disease will eventually be eliminated Healthcare will then shift to learning and applying these new technologies for prevention and immediate treatment, while assisting and supporting patients in raising their consciousness through new enlightened modalities. As there is no separation between body, mind, heart and and spirit, a shift in consciousness is necessary for all healing to be permanent. While the human vessel will continue to experience pain, long-term suffering and disease will no longer be a part of your experience.

Healthcare Centers

A new form of medical center, or rather wellness center, will first arise as cooperative endeavors between traditional well-care providers, what you presently refer to as medical workers, in association with alternative healers. Each will be supported in a mutual health benefit program, where all patient members of the center equally invest into the wellness center and its programs. Services are made available to each member on an as-needed basis. This wellness savings plan is similar to insurance; however, these savings funds benefit the members of the private medical care facility rather your present insurance concepts.

Each member will be investing in the wellness center itself and will receive the benefits of being a member. This group savings plan makes it possible for those who face emergency situations to have their needs met. In these private medical membership groups, pricing for services will not be based on insurance or government pricing. Rather, it will serve the best for all concerned and based on what is fair and reasonable, agreed upon by providers and members, and not on what any system indicates.

Insurance companies will transform from their present model. They will become medical savings plans with potential for personal growth year over year. These organizations will no longer control the medical and wellness industry or be tied to the pharmaceutical industry. Those organizations which do not evolve will no longer exist along with all other business concepts based in greed. All insurance and medical savings concepts will eventually become obsolete as human bodies become healthier and whole.

Your new wellness centers and models will not preclude medical professionals from also working elsewhere, in more traditional environments if they so choose. For a time, this may be necessary as you transition out of the old model and into the new. For those patients who seek a more traditional clinical environment, the old model will continue to exist until it becomes unnecessary.

Each new healing center model is a cooperation with practitioners openly sharing and supporting member patients thus ensuring all members receive the necessary whole-being wellness. Each clinic houses healing professionals with education and experience in allopathic, naturopathic, innovative techniques, energy healing, and spiritual wellness, working in harmony with each other, providing complementing services and mutual support in service to patients and each other.

Physical structures of the new healing centers will be made of glass, crystal, natural stone, and replenishable resources, and generously enhanced with green and growing plants, creating a healing oasis for a more harmonious environment with nature for maximum restoration of the whole being. No longer will patients feel trapped in sterile, unfeeling, clinical environments, shuffled into rooms, and treated numbers and names on a chart. These new wellness centers create a harmonious sense of calm. The healing begins the moment a member walks in the door and is met with love.

The wellness centers themselves will be modeled utilizing sacred geometry. At first, the concept of using circles rather than squares for creating structures such as school buildings and medical centers may feel uncomfortable for many, as they are stretched out of their boxes and comfort zones. For some, it may feel like a waste of space. However, circles offer a superior environment for energetic flow. This holds true within a medical setting as well as education, business, housing, and community environments.

Within each well-care center, a central hub will welcome each member patient, and every patient is treated with love, dignity, and respect. No one will be treated as less worthy than anyone else. All previous concepts used for labeling humans as less-than in any way will become extinct and all that will remain is healing the whole being.

Wellness Center Models

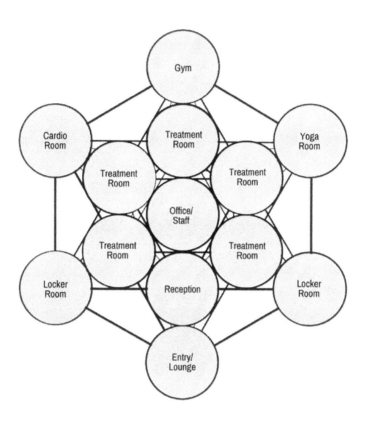

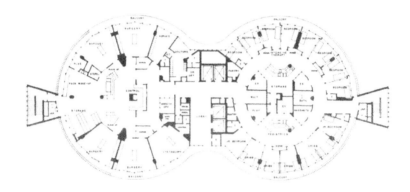

System 3. Environment

Earth is one of the most beautiful planets in the universe. Her life-giving capabilities ensure all beings on her body are nourished and supported. You are all made of her and her love for you is infinite. From her you have come and to her you will all return. Many of you are beginning to remember your collective mother and reconnect your heart to hers. You are no longer willing to tolerate the abuse to her body and all her creations.

Beyond Sustainability

Earth's ecosystems are the only true global systems and the only systems which will remain as a united plan for Earth and all her beings. Moving forward, the focus will shift from sustaining to replenishing. Sustainability of the status-quo and maintaining mere sustenance for the people, will be replaced with restoring the Earth to her grandeur for all life to thrive and prosper. The illusion of lack will disappear as all life is supported, nurtured, and brought to flourishing. Sustaining will be replaced with thriving.

All of Earth's environments and ecosystems will be cleaned up and restored to its original state as a plentiful garden of diversity. As your planet is restored there will no longer be harsh and cruel environments. Deserts will once again flourish, winds will calm, water will flow freely, the skies will clear, and balance will be returned. The library of the Universe held on the Earth realm will be abundant with life once again. Many seeds of life thought to be extinct will be restored in accordance with what is best for all life on Earth.

The emergence of new techniques will make it possible to clean and restore the oceans, while technologies presently used to manipulate weather conditions will be reversed and used to restore Earth's ecosystems. New modes of transportation will be created which no longer require fuel sources or electrical grids. New biodegradable plastics and fabrics will be created which are no longer dependent on the oil and chemical industries and cause no harm to the planet or her beings. Your world will shift from brown and barren to green and growing. All life will flourish and prosper as all life is intended.

Earth's entire food processes will shift from how food is presently grown, distributed, sold, and consumed. There will be an end to big-box businesses and corporate conglomerates. The global empires of greed will be dismantled. There will be a reemergence of growing groups working in cooperation with each other to support the highest good for all concerned.

Human Habits

Dining-in, eating smart, and communing with family and friends over home-prepared food will become more cherished than dining out among strangers. Restaurants will be expected to compost all food waste and will only have access to food products which are local, fresh, organic, and healthy. The focus will shift from what is easy and most profitable to what is best.

Existing fast-food chains, other than those which promote wellness, will eventually cease to exist. "Sourced local" will become the normal practice for all retail and food-based businesses, reducing the need for fuel consumption in the transportation industry. "Sourced local" provides for mutual support within communities while also reducing the need for factories and bringing an end to factory pollution and human enslavement. As focus shifts from quantity of goods to quality of life, the desire for anything other than "sourced local" will fall by the wayside.

The disease of consumption in the human mind and on the body of Earth is coming to an end. The desire for endless consuming and wasting of the planet and her resources will become a memory of the past. It will be a story of how humans used to live before they awakened and remembered who they are. All of humanity will love and honor the sacredness of your collective Mother Earth, and you will work in harmony to restore her to her fullest potential.

Unifying

All of you, every being on Earth, will begin to see that you were never separated or divided from each other. You will recognize yourselves as one human family on this one planet you share as your collective home. Competition of any kind will discontinue to exist as you pool your concepts and resources in cooperation with each other for the greatest good of the whole world.

Together you will clean and restore the oceans until they are again teaming with life. You will clean up the surface of Earth and re-green all her landscapes. The lakes, rivers and streams will be crystal clean and purified through your cooperative efforts. The skies will be so blue and clear you can almost see the stars by day. Together you will celebrate each other's genius as you unify to restore all of Earth's eco-systems Yes, even the planet herself will celebrate your successes.

In all your innovations and across all platforms, you will keep the ecosystems in mind, always asking yourselves, "What is the present impact on Earth and what will be its impact on the unforeseeable future?" This will play a primary role in all your decision making as you move through your creation revolution out of the old constructs of limitation and into a whole new world where everything becomes possible for everyone.

System 4. Agriculture

Earth is vibrant and full of life as the library of the Universe. Some life has been lost over time, and yet, nothing is ever truly lost. She is entering a renewal cycle and will be fully restored. This restoration comes through your hands as the caretakers of Earth. There is more than enough land and potential for growth to generously support all life on Earth.

Earth Domain

As you begin to comprehend that human dominion over Earth, as spoken of in your ancient texts, means to be in care of her and her beings rather than to dominate over, your focus will shift from control to care. You will change all your approaches to how your food is grown, cultivated, treated, and harvested, always keeping in mind the nourishment and wellbeing of all things.

This change requires humankind to reconsider all agricultural methodologies to restore Earth's bounty and work together to ensure all of life thrives. All concepts of agriculture will shift from making money to ensuring that all of life prospers. Factory farming and corporate ranching will become bygone concepts. Farmers and ranchers will work in harmony with each other, in cooperation, feeding animals what they naturally eat, while growing and fertilizing farms the most natural way.

The use of growing corn to feed cattle and farm animals will come to an end, as this is neither healthy for the animal or the environment. Subsidizing crops to keep a system of false nutrition alive for the sake of feeding deep pockets over feeding hungry bellies of people and animals will no longer be acceptable. Rather, farmers will be supported in growing plant diversity. Holistic and back-to-nature growing practices will shift the soil from nutrient-depleted to nutrient-dense, while also cleaning excess carbons from the air and returning them to the Earth field where they sustain life.

Agriculture will shift from tilling the soil to reenergizing it. There will be a change in consciousness from the one-crop mindset to growing multi-diversity plant life. Each farm will have a Garden of Eden appearance, teeming with life and plant culture. Flowers, vegetables, nuts, and fruits will all grow in harmony with each other as nature intended. This diversification of plants creates the biodiversity needed for soil to regenerate itself.

Cattle yards will vanish and be replaced by free-roaming cattle, where they will eat their natural food source, ensuring healthier production. Farmers will see the advantage of letting livestock and fowl eat in their fields as another way ranchers and farmers work together for mutual support. Allowing animals to graze on gardens and crops after the growing season allows for natural aeration of the soil, natural composting, and reduction of waste. This natural aerating, composting, and fertilizing of free-roaming animals, rather than their meat and milk, is their greatest gift to the world. Animals will be seen as collaborators in the New Earth creation, rather than as pests, problems, or merely profit. These new practices will restore the carbon balance and re-soil the planet.

You will begin to understand how the biodiversity of nature works within its own container to grow new life, rather than stifle the biodiversity through chemical controls and contamination. The chemical industry, which has taken over the food industry, will be removed from all food processes. This practice of placing chemicals into every aspect of the food chain will no longer be acceptable as it is proven harmful to all life on Earth. Chemicals will remain only for the purpose of creating compounds which restore Earth and full human potential until it is no longer necessary, and humanity outgrows it.

As your bodies, and all life on Earth evolves from carbon to crystalline, there will no longer be a desire to harm or eat the flesh of another being. You will have outgrown the hunter and gather phase of your collective evolution where hunting for animal flesh and gathering artificial food from supermarkets becomes a story from another bygone era. Eventually the desire to eat flesh of any kind will cease as your bodies outgrow this lower vibrational sustenance and all sentient beings will live symbiotically with humans without fear between them.

Nature's Way

Grow your fields and gardens the way nature intended. It may feel less productive as the farming industry was created for mass production. Yet as humanity changes its values, mass production and consumption will be less valued than quality and accessibility of multiple food choices. Gone will be the days of single crops for massive distribution.

We suggest when growing your vegetables, flowers, herbs, and fruit they be naturally intermixed rather than in rows of linear crops. Allow weeds and grass to grow in the garden, rather than pulling them out. Grass retains moisture and some weeds are beneficial. Some weeds and flowers naturally deter bugs and help to maintain healthy crops. You will find the plants that work most harmoniously with each other, and with the soils and weather within your unique communities and surroundings.

Planting the garden in circles, rather than squares or rectangles, allows for easy access on all sides and can be more aesthetically pleasing. Some may even choose to grow their garden as part of a labyrinth, or in the shape of sacred geometry. Allow your mind to be creative and grow your gardens not limited by functionality, but rather as a work of heart. When planting your garden, imagine it the way nature grows, with plant variety and cross-pollination all working together in harmony.

Garden labyrinths can be beautiful as well as functional. We suggest planting a garden of diversity, intermixing breeds, and varieties of vegetation for a more natural approach to growth. Edible flowers, bug- and disease-resistant plants, vegetables, herbs, berries, fruit, and nut trees can all be grown in the same space and field to mutually support each other.

These are gardens for beauty as much as they are gardens for food. The more harmonious the garden vegetation, the more fruitful the garden will be and the life-giving energy each garden puts forth. Adding shade trees, resting benches, fountains, and streams add to both the beauty and purpose of each garden. This is where nature meets functionality. Combined with technology, these reimagined gardens can be more peaceful and fruitful than all gardens of the past.

In areas where the climate is colder, these gardens can be encased in clear greenhouses with sliding panels, allowing in fresh, clean air and sunlight as needed, and easily closing to extreme temperatures when necessary. Some will choose glass domes as greenhouses with skylights and open windows or even earthen domes which maintain optimum growing temperatures in all seasons. These designs allow for year-round growth without losing the beauty and experience of nature in harmony with nurture.

Some may choose to have their own home garden while others will choose to grow their food in a mutually supporting garden co-op or community. There is no right or wrong way to grow your food, rather, the emphasis is on self-accountability and mutual sufficiency. The more who focus on local mutual support rather than expecting large corporations to feed their every need, the quicker the large corporations will melt away and human beings will again inter-create the way your world was always intended to be.

Eventually, as you evolve, your new light bodies will have little need for nourishment, and you will no longer need or desire to choose between ending any plant or animal life to sustain another life. You will have access to replicators capable of replicating anything your hearts and tastebuds desire. These replicators can create food at its molecular structure, yes even your favorites dishes, without the need for killing or chemicals. It is all "Source Energy" configured to delight your senses.

Garden Models

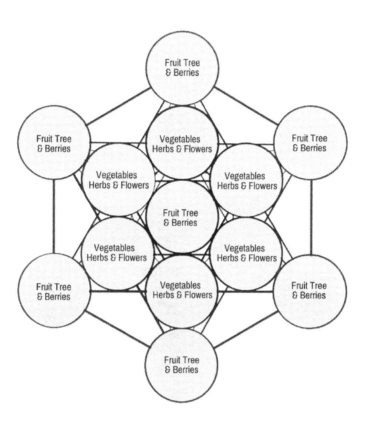

System 5. Governance

Humanity is growing up and outgrowing fear. At the soul level you have collectively agreed that you are finished with learning through the contrast of fear and darkness. You have chosen for Earth to be a planet of peace and prosperity for all. As fear subsides and eventually disappears, all constructs based in fear will disappear along with it.

Self-Governance

The need for governments will fade from existence as all people learn to self-regulate thorough love, and the need for leaders, external rules, and regulations are replaced with internal self-guidance. People will honor, support, and look after each other, not because they must, but because they choose to. As love supersedes fear, all concepts created in the old reality will no longer be necessary.

Without the role of fear in your everyday experience, all laws, prisons, and restraints will go by the wayside in the truth that all beings are worthy of respect. In the vibration of love, there is no desire to cause harm. You will all come to understand that harm against another is harm against yourselves, and harm against any other being is harm against the body of humanity and the planet. As fear dissipates from your existence, all who have been held in containment centers, or what some may call correction facilities, will be given the opportunity for deprogramming from their fear-based programs and become rehabilitated members of society.

There will be no need for prisons, police, or politics as all of humanity remembers their true compassionate, loving nature. When you remember who you are as divine beings having a human experience, you will no longer need external regulations of any kind as you will learn how to self-regulate within yourselves. You will be self-guided in all things by the love in your hearts rather than fear in your minds.

The concept of government, which translates to external control of the mind, will be shifting to self-governance. Some will argue that self-regulating and self-governance is impossible and cannot work. That is only because it has never been done, and precisely why it will work. All other forms of governance have proven futile and lead only to those who wish to exert power over others.

In the beginning, as you shift from your exising governmental programs and systems to self-governance models, you may find an interim balance between the two. External government systems may overlap for with internal guidance for a short period as you consider how to restructure what works best for each of you in your given environments.

Ending Old Structures

Peace forced through fear and control will be replaced by peace through loving choice. All constructs of power over are ending. All -ocracies, -archys, and -isms will be pulled from their mantles of fear. These labels exist only to create the grand illusion of division, disconnecting humanity from its true nature of oneness. Thus, monarchies, patriarchies, democracies, and theocracies will end as governance shifts out of some above others and against-ness toward your fellow beings. Eventually capitalism, socialism, racism, nationalism, and every other device for control will go by the wayside, and all will be replaced with humanitarianism.

Humanitarianism brings out the best in humanity as it brings to the forefront the compassion existing in the love of all life. This is where the Divine Mother, the Sacred Feminine, resides in the heart of all humans as the Heart of Compassion. Through your compassionate hearts you will work together to unify in harmony to positively affect and change all life on Earth.

Regarding nationalism, which many of you are still concerned with. This will also go by the wayside. Some presently see their own nation as better than the rest, creating animosity toward other people and nations. That is the Nationalism which drives war and division. Loving your country, being patriotic and wanting what is best for those around you, while not at the expense of another country or nation, is often confused with Nationalism.

As you move through the transition phase from Old World to New Earth, countries will focus on restructuring and supporting their own people rather than supporting global systems which are greed disguised as generosity. Once nations are restored to provide for their own people, have positive leadership models, and liberated from the constraints of those who had wished for global governance and domination, all countries will begin working together in union for the greatest good of all life on Earth and the Earth herself. This One Earth Consciousness will supersede all previous concepts attempting to maintain order and control. There is no need for control where there is genuine love.

As this worldwide union of the heart grows to mutual and loving support, all fear and division between nations becomes nonexistent. This oneness and mutual acceptance will eventually include intergalactic visitors who will share in your unified space. There will be some who hold their national pride, not out of the need to protect their nation or the desire to take from other nations, but because it is the region of Earth they love most and feel most at home.

As one unified planet in heart and mind, all countries, and their borders, will become merely places people are from. As human beings move about the planet, free of constraints or controls, and all against-ness toward those in and from other countries will become another bygone. Rather, you will all celebrate each other's heritage and home with the same reverence you have for your own homes and heritage.

Humanity will begin creating alliances with a focused purpose of creating conscious, mutually supporting concepts rather than making demands on the old, outdated systems. This is not the same as one-world government where there is one overreaching entity made of political and financial leaders insistent on making the world a better place through one system of control. Rather, each nation will be recognized as a wholly sovereign entity, fully supporting its own people and cultures while being free of constraints from any global agenda.

All counties will work in harmony, creating a global alliance and working together with other alliances for the highest and greatest good of all concerned, creating a win/win/win for all life on Earth. This creates an interdependence of independent nations rather than continual codependence based on control and neediness. This interdependence allows all countries to thrive and mutually support each other, knowing they can depend upon each other, without being dependent on each other for survival. You will unwind your entanglements to interconnected systems and instead will come together in harmony and balance.

All forms of governance, yes, even at the global level, will be based on councils of representatives chosen by the people to represent them, and with no one person at the helm. All councils will communicate openly and freely with other councils from every nation and culture, to share best practices to determine what is best for their citizens, and the citizens of Earth. This will no longer be through any interest in controlling the people of Earth, but in the desire for all people to rise to their individual greatness for all of life to thrive and prosper.

Restructuring

As the governments of your world begin to collapse, each country will decide how to restructure its systems in a way which better serves all people within their society. Some countries will find themselves with an interim government under the care of forward focused and well-meaning military until new models of governance are created. Other countries will choose to no longer be governed and move directly into forms of self-governance and cooperation, meeting their own societal needs and preferences.

In those cities, states, and countries where the people determine they need to be governed, their model of governance will shift from control to service. All existing forms of government will crumble as all are based in control of human resources rather than in servant-leadership. All concepts of political parties and preferences will no longer play out as human beings all come to accept each other as "we" and choose to no longer be divided amongst themselves.

The governance of each city, state, and country will be fully reconstructed to serve the wellbeing of the people and will no longer be manipulated through corporate or partisan interests. There will only be volunteer positions, free of any form of financial compensation and egoic pride. These will be positions in service to the whole and held accountable by the people for all choices made on behalf of the people. No decisions will be made for the people without the people's full, conscious consent.

All positions of governance, from the local to the international level, will contain term limits to ensure no one becomes full of themselves and are not easily swayable by money or power. Term limits ensure continual turnover of each role, allowing more individuals to participate in learning leadership skills and being of service to all concerned.

The concept of party systems will become another bygone concept as this only means to divide and conquer those under its supposed care. Rather, all those elected by the people will represent the people's desires. Those who choose to represent the people will do so out of love for the people. The people will choose representatives from within their own demographic, with representatives from every walk of life: gender, age, creed, and shade of skin, chosen by the people for their proven integrity, words, and deeds, rather than by political affiliation, putting an end to all arguments of non-representation and divisiveness. All representation will only be in concern for the highest and greatest good of all people. This will require heartfelt communication, compassionate listening, and a genuine desire to serve what is best for all.

The ancient concept that some people exist to control and make decisions for those beneath them will finally cease from your human story. This old story was created in the darks contrast to prevent the masses from recognizing their own inner guidance. As you remember how to lead your own lives, all external leadership will be based in heart-centered service and mutual support, with none above others. The need for some to control others is based in fear and as fear dissipates from the human experience, there will be no need nor desire for control.

Leadership Framework

All concepts of leadership will be based on councils rather that pyramids. One man or woman at the top presiding over all others will be replaced with mutual support and interconnectedness. Interlocking circles will become the leadership model. "What is best for all life on Earth?" will become the new framework of all Earth-based systems. Each council is represented by a circle with core leadership represented by the innermost circle.

Organizations, programs, and systems determined to require leadership will experience a new framework for how leadership is represented. Core leadership will be comprised of a trinity, rather than one individual at the top commanding all others, ensuring no one person makes decisions for the whole. All three members of the core will work together in unity and harmony, in service to those within their dominion of care, and for the greatest good of all.

An example of this trinity on a national government scale may be a fusion of existing partisan models with a non-partisan model. A president or prime minister for example, will be independent of any political party and play the role of neutrality with one vice president from each party until at which time party politics dissolve and melt away. Other countries may find a neutral third party with a leader from the neutral party to be the best choice for leadership, creating an equal three-party system, until all parties and leadership models are no longer needed.

Some counties may choose to completely restructure their voting system to ensure a more equitable vote for their leadership model. In the United States for example, until the political system becomes redundant and unnecessary, you may choose for your senate to be comprised of two members from each state, and your congress comprised of one member from each grid as the country's voting is distributed into equal-sized grids to avoid the manipulation of what you call gerrymandering. A third voting entity may be created which is comprised of representative members from each walk of life:

young, old, rich, poor, male, female, Black, White, and so on until groups are created to represent the people as elegantly and fairly as possible. As the country is divided into voting grids for more fair representation, rather than by states, each small grid represents the interests of the people rather than state preferences. This prevents some states from bulldozing over others with differing ideas. This may also be used for presidential and vice-presidential elections, with one electoral vote coming from each grid, thus allowing for all people's votes to be equally represented. This is power to the people rather than power to politics.

These same models where all people's interests are equally represented may also be used in other forms of leadership such as corporations, organizations, cities, states, and countries, and may even be used for international representation and the betterment of humanity. This is where humanity breaks free from government over people, places, and things to governance by and for the people.

There will be transparency in all things as all leadership and representative meetings are televised live, streaming to all people affected by the meetings. This is where global technology shines. All who choose to watch and ensure they are being adequately represented are free to view and participate.

Nothing will be withheld from the people and all decisions will be made in full disclosure for all constituents.

It must be this way for infinite and mutual trust of all people everywhere. When there is nothing to hide, there is no reason not to embrace full transparency. Yes, this will be a stretch for those who have been sweeping their actions under rugs and hiding their secrets in proverbial closets. This will no longer be acceptable behavior. All people deserve complete transparency from those they chose to lead them, and they shall have it.

As governments are slimmed to leadership roles only consisting of non-paid positions, taxes will be removed from economics as all beings are seen through the eyes of true equality. There will be no tax benefits to corporations and those at the top will no longer squeeze every drop of loopholes from the systems to benefit themselves. There will no longer be syphoning of money to feed greedy pockets from the earnings of honest people. Greed is based in fear and the belief that there is lack. In truth, there is no lack. There is only the illusion of lack and a desire to control existing and future resources. Without fear, green and the need for control disappears.

New concepts will allow individuals to pursue more fulfilling interests outside of government jobs, and programs will be put into place for supporting individuals who are unable to financially support themselves. These have offered a false sense of support and security as governments siphon off the top to meet the demands of special interests while blaming the people for the reason there isn't enough for everyone. This is nothing new. Tax the poor to feed the rich is only recently disguised as caring for the poor. This too is being reformulated to rebalance the playing field of Earth.

Every person will have their needs met without the middleman of systems, governments, and controlling overseers. All projects and programs will be supported for the people, and by the people, as giving to those less fortunate, and mutual support supersedes government constructs. Those in need will be given hand-ups rather than hand-outs, feeding their desire for creativity, self-sufficiency, and being a valued member of society. Al beings regardless age, education, gender, shade of skin or country of origin will be treated with equality, honor, dignity, and respect.

Taxation and Social Programs

Collapsing one reality without laying the groundwork for a new reality would create chaos and we have found that easing the transition is easier on the human heart. During the transition phase, there may be some taxation to facilitate the change, just as there will be some government to calm the process.

Income taxes will be replaced by other forms of taxation, until all taxation goes by the wayside. Taxes based on income creates imbalance and less vs more, promoting greed and less-than-ness. Rather, income tax will be replaced with a flat, as low as possible, sales tax ensuring every individual from the bottom to the top, regardless of national or corporate status, all equally contribute, thus mutually supporting each other and the services provided from tax collection. Taxes have never been necessary to create cohesive societies and you will all come to recognize this. New programs and projects will be put into place which provide mutual support and cooperation rather than through government oversight and control.

Sales tax will not be applied to necessities for living such as fresh food and shelter, and unnecessary on any previously owned item upon which tax has already been paid. This idea of bleeding the people in everything they do, and telling them it is for their own good, will stop. This is akin to punishing a child, taking their allowance to pay for adult issues, and then telling the child it is in their best interest. Fresh food will not be taxed, yet packaged, processed and restaurant food may be. This will encourage individuals to seek out healthier and more natural options rather than supporting corporate conglomerates which in themselves are a dying concept.

For the interim, where taxes continue to be collected, governments, from cities to countries, will become transparent in how they spend the people's money. Regular reports will be provided to the people in complete acceptance that the people are shareholders and have personal stake in how their money is spent. This is the opposite of your present systems where the people are assets of your governments rather than co-owners.

Again, all forms of government will eventually be replaced with self-governance. The concept of voting for leaders will be short-lived. All concepts of leadership will be replaced by mutual representation for the greatest good of the whole, knowing every person is capable of self-regulation. All government models will eventually fade as human beings learn self-governance is the only necessary governance and all operation is cooperation.

All politics and any concepts of some above others and the need for some to represent others will become a thing of the past as all people are able to represent themselves and their communities. All voting will shift from voting for people to voting only on issues and services which serve the highest and greatest good of all concerned.

Governance Models

This model of the United States government is one model for consideration and inter-creation. All departments and roles will be phase out as they are deemed no longer necessary for genuine service to the people.

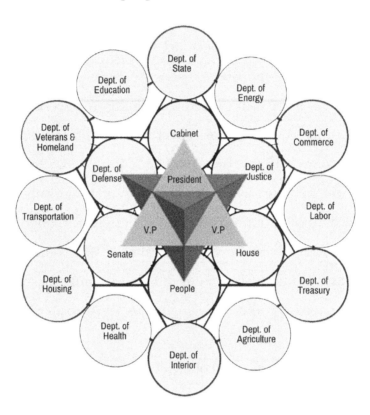

System 6. Economics

The economies of yesteryear are failing to thrive. They have been built on quicksand and have no solid foundation to stand on. The systems based on fear have always been volatile, constantly needing to be shored up and stabilized because they were not built on the rock of love. Greed is unsustainable and must constantly be fed to keep it alive. The monster of greed is dying, slipping back into the dark nothingness from whence it came. Fear will no longer syphon from the people to feed the minds of greed as humanity now sees how the game has been played. You will choose share economies rather than continuing to supply your slave economies.

Slave Economy

Everything you believe about money and economics is about to change. Nothing is the way so many of you have been taught to believe. While some of you are aware of how money and your systems have been used to enslave humanity, many of you are not. Trust Dear Ones that all of you will become aware and in this awareness you will uncreate what was created by those who wished to enslave you in the disguise of service and support.

Money is a temporary solution as a solvent for the issues at hand. It will become freely available for everyone as you free yourselves from the systems which have become engorged with your earnings. The fat cats at the tables controlling your daily sustenance will be forced to share and you will no longer need to beg at their feet for meager wages. You will no longer experience the monopoly money now floating between accounts to feed the overseer's buffet while the masses fight over the scraps left by their task masters. Your concepts of money, until money is no longer necessary, will be liberated from governmental, banking, and corporate controls.

All systems of enslavement will be ending. Humanity will be set free to pursue self-sufficiency through self-determination and free enterprise. Your systems of financial control, presently promoted to you as systems of support, are unnecessary when all of you thrive. Sovereignty, interdependence, mutual support and cooperation will be the new economics, and prosperity-for-all the new flow of currency. No longer will anyone feel deprived of resources or reliant on services which serve some and not others.

Free Enterprise

All your present industries are based on the industriousness of the people, on the backs of hard-working men and women in the misrepresentation that jobs working for corporate conglomerates are necessary for survival. This is yet another way the monster of greed is fed by those unaware of the roles being played. In your new world where love supersedes all else, corporations based solely on greed will eventually cease to exist. All corporate and financial empires will crumble and all systems which support those empires will be dismantled as humanity is liberated from its enslavement.

The endless cycle of break one's back for consumption of Earth's resources is a cycle that will come to an end. All corporate entities dependent on the cycle of consumption will begin to collapse and be replaced by organizations which focus only on real solutions for all life on Earth and assisting the recreation of Earth. The addiction to consume, consume, consume will be replaced with replenish, replenish, replenish. You will all stand tall, no longer bending at will of others, knowing the role you each play in restoring and replenishing the Earth.

Corporate empires will be brought to their knees and replaced by organizations with a sincere desire to be of service to all life on Earth. The concept of corporations existing for the purpose of selling out or buying out will be replaced with creating businesses which serve a higher purpose. Many corporations will be dismantled altogether as they do not serve what is best for humanity. Some corporations will be reduced to dust and others will be broken up into individual free-enterprise pursuits. In essence, chopping up the sharks to free the minnows eaten up in the frenzy to rule the world. Many smaller companies may decide to separate themselves from the parent corporations which brought them into their corporate empire and will wish to be set free. Others may simply slip into the memory of what once was as you leave the past behind.

There will be a restoration of free enterprise where individuals and organizations work together in mutual support and in cooperation for the betterment of the community, and for shared outreach. Businesses not based in love will fail to thrive because human hearts will no longer support anything less. Purpose over profit will become the new sustainable practice of how all things are done.

As the concept of jobs goes by the wayside in lieu of self-reliance, corporate structures will no longer be necessary. The days of humans being locked up in wooden boxes by night and cubicles in tall metal buildings by day is over. Human beings will be free to pursue their dreams and do work they love, for the love of their work. They will no longer bow down to taskmasters and work simply because there is money in it. If it doesn't empower their heart and feed their spirit, they will find other work with meaning and purpose. Work will not be work, rather it will be play, and the hours invested will be by choice rather than obligation.

Corporations will be returned to the original intent of cooperations for the purpose of inter-creating projects, products, and services. There will be no need for overseers as all projects will come from the heart rather than from greed, and all communication will come through a desire for mutual support rather than some above others. While there may still be some human management involved with project management, it will be with the complete understanding that all roles are equally valued and those with more experience and understanding lend a hand to those who are less experienced, thus everyone rises.

Expect your current concepts of investing in companies to also go by the wayside as investing in invisible stock in a market based on greed will no longer serve anyone. It has only served to make the rich richer and the poor poorer and is a false sense of security and entitlement. It puts profits over people and profits at whatever means necessary, making false money for the corporate owners and their stockholders. Those corporations boast about how much they care while only caring about their bottom lines, and cry over small losses in the international marketplace while their consumers suffer from lack of support and shoddy products. That time is near an end, and it will be good riddance for humanity.

Investing in companies will return to the way it was always meant to be and that is, investing from the heart. Those who have the means to invest will invest in companies they love and believe in rather than companies with the greatest potential for financial return. They will no longer gamble on brands because of their ticking stock, but rather the ticking of their heart and their purpose on the planet.

Investing in business, for those who have the financial wherewithal to invest, will bypass the present stock and bond system based on greed and manipulation. Investors will be invested in companies where they have real stock in the concept's success, and wholeheartedly believe in the products and services provided by the companies. Investors will no longer invest for the purpose of growing their portfolio, but in growing the satisfaction that comes with watching another person thrive.

Eventually, human beings will outgrow money altogether, as a new way of having their needs met becomes created. In the interim, new money, money based on Earth assets rather than human indebtedness, will begin to set all of humanity free from working for mere sustenance. Human beings will live for a life they love, rather than live for work merely to sustain life.

Heart Work

All concepts of corporate leadership, from the top down, will be replaced with mutual support and mutual respect for all. Each member of the team will be recognized for their individual contribution and insights, no longer looked up to in worship or down upon as servants, as all gifts and all beings are recognized and valued, and competition becomes a thing of the past.

All association to ownership of human potential and control of human beings as corporate resources will be recognized for its absurdity. Human beings are not meant to be caged or owned, even in the disguise of business ownership. Businesses will no longer be based on the industriousness of humans as a resource but rather on the expansion of human hearts through their creativity, and contentment. Businesses and individuals will begin to utilize the circular model as they see this as a more balanced and cohesive way of going about their work. Individuals will see themselves at the center of their pursuits, holding balance in every area of their lives, rather than at the top attempting to control it all.

Companies will be created as circular structures with a core individual holding the organization together, as a wheel with spokes rather than the pyramid. The pyramid (a representation of the masculine) and the cone-shaped vessel (a representation of the feminine) will work in harmony for the betterment of all life on Earth. All business concepts and structures will focus on authentic balance and equality in the workplace.

Humanity will be liberated from the concept of working for others and striving for a paycheck and will experience being rewarded for following their innate gifts and the desires of their hearts. While some may choose to work under the guidance of others toward a mutual outcome, every person on the team will be self-employed and self-responsible. There will be a return to everyone following their craft, expanding their gifts, and loving their work, rather than making career choices based on income. The striving for bigger, better, and more will shift to striving for inner bliss and personal peace. Professions and lifestyle choices will be made from the heart, and will follow inner purpose, rather than based on any form of financial or external expectations.

All people will be encouraged to follow their inspiration and purpose, to follow their creative bliss, rather than getting a job. Working for someone else just to pay the bills will become a thing of the past, as it does not fulfill the heart. Those who prefer to work for others will seek out projects and opportunities which align with the desires of their heart, rather than having a job just to have a job. Corporate cubicles and enslavement systems will die away as they have all been built on feeding those at the top.

Businesses will no longer put profits over people in the absolute awareness that profits are a natural consequence of genuine, loving service. Thriving businesses will give to those in their domain of care in a fair and generous manner, while those who create the business concepts have no need for greed. The days of buying and collecting needless things to be accepted in the right circles, and to feed an endless appetite for anything new, will go by the wayside as the joy of being of service and helping the world become a better place, fills all empty hearts.

The need for hierarchy and desire for titles will evaporate as the ego no longer needs feeding and preservation. It will be calmed in the assurance that all is well and there is nothing to fear. There will be no greed, as the truth is abundance is freely available. All who desire to control Earth's prosperity and her people will be brought to their knees and shown the error of their ways. Some will change their hearts and turn to service and others will fade into the shadows and be forgotten. Their legacies will be stricken from the record and stories left in the ashes of the past.

Sharing as Currency

Currency is a flow of energy. Money as a form of currency is used as a means of exchange in gratitude for services rendered, although many of you have forgotten to give and receive in gratitude. That too is changing. The more you use it through gratitude the more it will grow and expand. As money becomes less important as a means of exchange, other forms of energy exchange and appreciation will replace it. New technologies will eventually replace any need for money as all needs will be met without the need for financial exchange.

Money is a gift from the Earth to be used as a gift from the heavens. As all beings begin to see themselves as worthy of this extraordinary gift and learn to be wise stewards of it, there will no longer be a need for it because you will outgrow it. Money will continue to exist as the primary means of exchange until it is phased out and replaced with a process far more prosperous.

Rather than simply using money for exchange, trading goods and services will be more greatly encouraged. They appreciate the true value of the goods and services rendered rather than being dependent on the financial value placed on them. More and more emphasis will be placed on share economies, trading goods, combined community services and new cooperative models.

Money and Banking

Banking systems, government reserves, lending for profit, and credit systems will vanish. These deliver a false sense of security and the illusion of buying happiness while creating a continual cycle of indebtedness and inflated economy. These financial concepts will go by the wayside as all systems shift to support all people. Every person will be free to follow their heart without financial constraints or economic concerns, and beyond all government and corporate controls.

Banks, current structures for holding and lending other people's money, will be replaced by cooperative holding centers. Private holding vaults will be a place for holding valuables and making like-minded and mutually beneficial relationships rather than places to grow and lend money for some and not others. The past banking practices of feeding those who own the banks and financial institutions while only providing small stipends to members for safekeeping of their money is near its end.

All holding places will be of mutual and equal benefit of all as membership-based associations and models. Members may choose to keep currency, precious metals, and valuables in this shared and highly secure space, while holding each other accountable for the greatest good of all concerned. Members may also choose to support each other's ventures in a cooperative and mutually agreed upon alignment between specific parties and unassociated to the overall membership.

Imagine if you will, as some of our dear Earth beings have visualized, Saint Germain, the guardian of Earth's prosperity programs, standing as a holographic image at the doorway, inviting you into your savings places with the walls adorned with sacred geometry and spiritual protection. Yes, prosperity is a spiritual practice, meant to support all life, and will do so in the hands of love.

Less is More

People will become more concerned and compassionate and will no longer be tempted with consumption and consumerism. "Less is more," will be the new mantra over the old "he who has the most toys wins," "keeping up with the Joneses," and "got to have the newest tech." All of that will be replaced with the truth that happiness cannot be bought or stolen. It will all be replaced with, "How can all of us have the best of everything?" not from a materialistic standpoint but from a genuine desire for everyone to be their best selves, and for all of life to thrive.

Less equates to more. Less drama equals more inner peace as drama tears at the heart. Less competition equals more accomplishment as cooperation is the natural human state. Less "stuff" equals more serenity, as clutter leads to confusion. Less overeating leads to more health. Less doing allows for more being. This "less is more" understanding will lead to the end of a desire of needless things to fill the void created by fear, and rather, understand the more they let go of what they don't really need, the less stress they feel. The less of a drive there is to consume, the more time is valued, and the long hours of working for others just to pay the bills will halt, never to be picked back up again.

Time is your most valued currency, not in the way of charging each other for time, but the real value of time for friends, family, and doing what each person loves most. You will all seek out more time for happiness through pursuits of the heart rather than trading your precious gift of time for pursuits of material goods or giving your time in exchange for money at the hands of others who in the past have determined your supposed worth. You will all come to see that your worth is inherent and limitless, and money is nothing more than a resource for transformation.

Financial Choices

All financial choices will be made based on what feels best rather than what one can afford or should have as a means of following the crowd. Some will choose a simpler lifestyle free of the concerns of maintaining vast responsibilities, while others will choose a complex lifestyle and the responsibilities that come with leadership. All of it comes from following one's heart and alignment with each soul's purpose.

Expect the return of open markets and cooperative business models. Corporate stores will be replaced by mutually supporting businesses where creators, farmers and small-scale manufacturers provide goods and services directly to consumers. Without all the layers of middlemen between the creator and the consumer, which makes pricing prohibitive yet disguised as a better deal, customers will find supporting the brands they love as simple as loving those who supply the brands.

They will once again get to know their local farmer, grocer, butcher, tailor, healer, and soap maker and so on, as community becomes more important and invaluable than big store convenience and big box brands. Those too are a dying concept as human beings decide to support each other rather than the large conglomerates who make billions on the backs of the people.

Everyone will begin to understand and consciously utilize the universal Law of Circulation. They will use the concept of circulation, with love in all things, as a new methodology for collective progress. Within the Law of Circulation, nothing is ever depleted or wasted, rather it expands and all of life thrives. Through circulation there is continual creation, reciprocation and contribution.

Corporate Structure Model

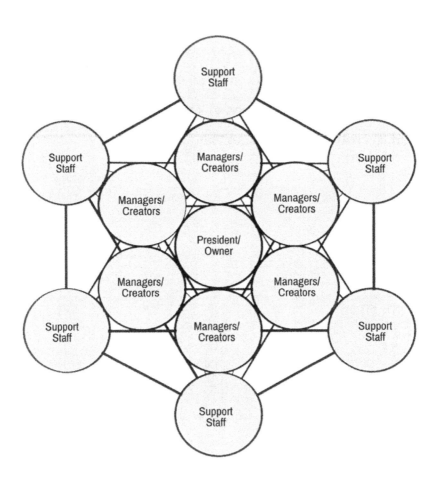

System 7. Military

The concept of weapons, tools of death and harm, and a belief that one must defend themselves from an external threat came to Earth along with fear. Prior to your agreement of souls to learn through the contrast, there was only peace and harmony between all beings. As your planet is restored to paradise, all tools of harm will disappear, never to be picked back up again.

Outgrowing Fear

Humanity will outgrow its co-dependency with fear. Understand that your own fear fuels the old paradigm of conquer and control. As you shift your personal beliefs from fear to love, with it will end the old constructs built on a foundation of fear. The apparent need for defence comes from fear and self-preservation, rather than trusting in your hearts and the love which all things are made of. The more of you who focus on love, harmony, and unity the sooner your lust for weapons will dissipate. What you presently recognize as the Military Industrial Complex will cease to exist along with all desire for weapons of any kind. Human beings will no longer see each other as enemies and instead will put down their armaments of offense and defence and will embrace each other as one Earth Family.

Your weapons and war machines will be melted down and destroyed, or repurposed and turned into useful tools for creation and rehabilitation. The stories of wars and weapons will go into the books of your past and you will forget the meaning of hate. Your posterity will pause in concern, and they will wonder how it was ever possible for human beings to choose hate. They will be amazed at your belief that some are more deserving than others and your insistence on destroying others who are not like you. In the forthcoming days you will celebrate unity as all of you choose to lay down your weapons of fear and embrace each other in love and mutual support. As you become willing to put down your armaments of destruction and take up arms with each other, you will find solidarity and the freedom you seek.

Choosing Love

You will come to see that all offense and defence is a game of division created in fear, and you will choose to no longer play that old game of compete, conquer, and control. Rather than focusing on how you must defend yourselves and your families from an oncoming slaughter or overarching controls, you will focus instead on real solutions which cause all desire for bigger and better weapons of destruction to disappear. Your unified focus will dismantle the controls without one weapon being lifted.

As you let go of your lust affairs with your guns and bombs, understanding they cannot and will not save you, you will find a greater strength and will within yourselves. You will see that weapons of any kind further flame the fires of hate and against-ness. These tools were created in a world based on fear and for the sole purpose of causing harm and death. They must be treated with that understanding and respect the power they yield over life and death.

As more of you unify in one heart and one purpose, the need to defend yourselves against each other will dissipate and disappear. As you make unity your primary focus your world will unify. Rather than rallying the troops to carry guns and battle arms, you will rally each other with the truth that love conquers all. With love, all things are possible, and love will prevail. When put down your weapons, and along with them the fear that you are alone, you will be welcomed with loving arms by your Galactic Family. They will teach you innovative technologies for peace rather than war and you will be invited to travel among the stars.

System 8. Development

As you develop and expand more love in your hearts and the controls of fear fade from your minds, you will begin to see your true preferences, wants and desires more clearly. All your physical developments, structures, landscapes and living environments will shift to follow suit.

Cityscapes

City centers will become garden centers. Genuine green living and green business will replace the outdated "green washing" and "virtue signaling" many individuals and corporations have used in the past to elicit trust while not putting their works behind their words. Those were empty words driven by greed and have no real heart. Inauthenticity will no longer be tolerated and those not aligned with their words will be disinvited from the New Earth creation process. Genuine care for all people and the planet will supersede narratives of anything less.

As humans move away from corporate empires and into self-sufficiency, many existing corporate structures will be imploded, dissolved, and turned into green space as buildings become a waste of space and needless reminders of the past. Only those which are necessary for telling the story of how humans used to live will be chosen to remain.

In this whole new world, anything that isn't beautiful simply won't exist, and anything considered ugly will no longer penetrate the planet. She will no longer tolerate4 the ugliness between people or the devastation to her body. Any structures which remain will become green buildings. This is not the same as your present usage of this term which used to describe those buildings with solar structures or self-generated electricity. In this new greening of structures, buildings will be in concert with nature. Their sides and rooftops will thrive with green and living life, all planted with trees, vines, vegetation, and flowers. They will no longer be harsh and cold metal and cement boxes, but rather create harmonic presence with the scene around them.

Architecture will become a new art form of both function and nature. This is where you blend evolution with devolution. Anything that doesn't evoke beauty and gratitude will be removed from your scenes. And yes, cleanup will be a snap with the technologies which leave no footprint behind and allows for immediate beautification of space.

In the desire for inner peace and greater self-sufficiency, the face of business and housing will move out of congested cities and into more open spaces. Cityscapes will shift from centers for human enslavement to centers for real and genuine connection. Tall buildings created for the purpose of greed and human management, except those which are chosen for their beauty and elegance, will be removed and be replaced with graceful centers for meetings of enlightened minds and liberated hearts. They will be utilized for social gatherings, loving inter-creation, and heartfelt communication in joy and celebration. City centers will become peace gardens.

Working Spaces

As the Earth is renewed and becomes more resource-full, people will spread out into intentional communities or have more self-expansion space. While there may be some who prefer smaller spaces and appreciate close quarters living, this will no longer be a choice made in economics but rather by personal preference. Individuals will all work from home or in mutual working spaces, doing what they love, rather than commuting to corporate buildings, away from their families and slaving for a taskmaster. Some may choose to continue working outside the home in a more structured environment. Work environments will feed the heart through focusing on beauty, wellbeing, and creation in the truth that creation and personal satisfaction makes for a more rewarding bottom line.

While cooperations may choose to have physical, central locations for cocreating and personal connection, they will not be spaces for controlling and overseeing employees. Work becomes joy when all work is in service to all people. Making money for the sake of making money for some to have bigger, better, and more out of the fear that some deserve more than others, will be replaced by personal choice. In a reality based in love, generosity will become the new face of business.

Community and cooperation will take precedence over all else and will also include worldwide community and cooperation. Competition is based in fear and the belief that some must lose for others to win. As fear subsides, competition will also go by the wayside. No longer will there be a few men and women at the top who compete for control of human and natural resources. They will be stripped of their hierarchy or face putting their money where their mouths are.

Companies can no longer spout how important the Earth is to them while siphoning her resources and contributing to her demise. Those who have caused the greatest harm on humanity and the Earth will be stripped of their entitlements and their assets given to those who will use the reward to benefit all life on Earth. This leveling of the playing field will make it possible for the entire Earth landscape to shift out of the hands of fear and into the hands of love.

New Communities

Communities will shift out of convenience and into intentional. New communities will spring forth across the Earth landscape. Each of these will be mutually supportive of all members, free of all overarching dogma and expectations of a few over the many. Communities will work in harmony with nature rather than continuing the demolition of it.

Expect a rise in alternative communities, not held together in boxes and grids. Rather, there will be an increase in unique designs including treehouse, dome-home, earthen, greenhouse and sacred geometry communities. Without any controls over natural resources, creativity is free to thrive. New homes will be constructed utilizing unconventional resources, including fused-colored recycled glass, ground coverings, stone, crystal, recycled wood, reused fixtures, repurposed plastic, hemp and so forth. There is no limit to human imagination when it is free to flourish.

Conscious communities will grow and develop with an emphasis on green space, natural beauty, self-sufficiency, and positive energy. They will be mutually supporting of all members with no governance of at the helm. Rather, each community member will be seen as mutually and equally beneficial to the whole and all will work in interdependence for the greatest good of all concerned.

The focus on new communities based in mutual support and combined purpose will drive new developments. All will have the spirit of love for each other and all life on Earth as the core of all creation and development. You will see a growth in communities dedicated to specific purpose, for example, artist communities, writer communities, garden communities and so one. Some will trade with each other, and some communities will be fully self-sufficient.

The desire for return to community will stimulate the human core of creativity and concepts of physical community will be reimagined. All this remodeling, recreating, and restructuring your human developments will come from the heart in concern for the highest and greatest good of all concerned, and each will be unique to those who choose to live in harmony and concert with each other.

Community Models

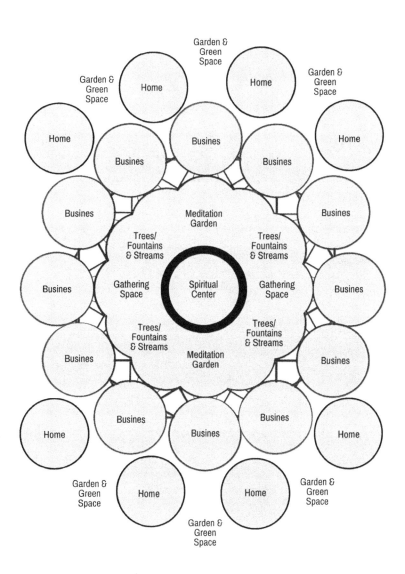

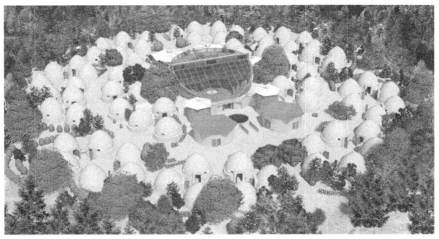

System 9. Family

Remembering that many of your ancient texts were written, compiled, and translated by men who wished to control humanity through fear, you are now able to deconstruct those old stories of war and ownership of others, and restore true stories of balance and harmony. In essence you will be adding her stories alongside his stories to see the whole picture of family and love at home within your own hearts. A rebalancing of the story will show your full potential and the expanded view of your human story.

Family Redefined

Humanity will need to accept that the old definition of family no longer serves what is best for all concerned. One man at the top is an old construct created in a reality based in fear. It was formed during a time when the belief that wombs and their creations were the property of men and that women were created to meet the needs of men. The truth is no person owns another and all beings were created for the love of each other.

Your roles as mates and beloveds are to mutually support each other as partners an inter-creators in all things. Your roles as parents and elders are to guide the younglings in your care to make the best and most loving choices for themselves and others on their path of life. They are not yours for coercion and control, and your happiness is not derived from their choices. They are family and in the world, you are creating, family extends beyond physical family to soul family. Your family includes your family of origin, family of choice, and the entire human family. As you come to recognize each other as divine beings having a human experience all concepts of ownership of each other will disappear.

Families will no longer be held together by government-sanctioned binds of matrimony and patriarchy but through your pledges of love. You will become each other's beloveds through terms of endearment rather than terms of ownership. Yes, this will be a challenge for many in the beginning as you learn to let go of constructs and allow each other to move more freely. And, in the genuine heart of love, there is no fear of love wandering away from you. The binds of love are more powerful than bonds of marriage contracts created and held together for legalities and taxation for principalities.

Matrimony was created as a business concept between men in your ancient history as contracts of ownership for the wombs of women on behalf of building the kingdoms of men. Only recently it evolved to a family business contract between husband and wife and then to a contract based on love. As women's minds, bodies and hearts become fully respected and restored to their place on the mantle alongside the masculine, and all beings are accepted as worthy of love, marriage contracts will no longer be necessary. All beings will be seen and respected with balance and absolute equality and with none above another.

Your spiritual bonds with each other will be tighter than any papers proving you belong to each other. While children will know where their homes are and where they are held most dear, they will also feel the loving support of others in their realm. The same holds true for your adult relationships. You will know and trust your hearts and stay in the beautiful communion of love with your soul mates and twin souls, rather than looking for fulfillment elsewhere. You will know that all love and fulfillment come from within, and all other beings reflect the love you grow within yourselves.

Sex solely for entertainment and without love and mutual honor will become another story of the past as you learn that you are your own source of love, and another being is not necessary to complete you. You will learn to guard your physical vessels and energy and share these only as you feel guided. In this wholeness within yourself, you will become magnetic to your energetic match and magnify each other in your loving resonance. This will become the new bond of family from which new life will spring forth.

The family unit will become a balance of masculine and feminine, (not necessarily man and woman) with parental figures creating a strong and stable home environment. As the original human blueprint is restored, gender confusion will come to rest. Every person will be at home with themselves, and humanity will more lovingly accept all humans for who they are. Gender bias, caste systems, racial tension, and all forms of human division will no longer exist. There will come a time when human beings will be astounded that any being was ever seen as unworthy of a fully loving and fully supported human experience.

The family unit is a circle of love where children are protected, nurtured, and respected for who they are rather than who parents desire or expect them to be. All paths will be acknowledged and accepted. This mutual respect, support, and understanding allow everyone in the family unit to thrive. This is not about allowing children to dictate their own lives, as all children need loving support and guidance, but to help children learn how to make the best choices free of coercion, expectation, and indoctrination. Children will be free to explore the wonder and lightheartedness that comes with being a child.

Conscious parenting in a conscious new world will allow children to grow, stretch and evolve into extraordinary human beings, unlimited by the fear of disapproval and lack of support. Parents will come to accept they do not own their children and will understand the role they play as guardian and guide in the personal evolution of each child.

Utilizing sacred geometry for establishing New Earth families, the parental relationship is at the core of the family unit as a trinity, with children being supported from within and seeing they are just as valuable to the family unit as their Earth guardians. In essence, each child experiences what many of you refer to as a holy trinity of divine child, father, and mother. Outer circles represent siblings, extended family, and community support for the child/parent unit. All systems ultimately exist to support the family unit and bringing up the next generation in a world where everything becomes possible through love.

Not everyone will feel compelled to have children and there will be no social pressure to do so. Those who choose to become parents will be emotionally supported by all. In a world where there is only love, honor, and respect, there will be no unwanted pregnancies or discarded children. Every life will be honored for the gift life is. Each child will be lifted and grow in the truth that every being is worthy of infinite love. Every being will be wrapped in the arms of unconditional love and supported by the infinite resources made available to all living kind.

Living Environment

Homes will be a gathering place for connection and personal growth. They will be a place of renewal and respite for the soul. A place for gathering friends, extended family, and personal community to come together in celebration, laughter, and delight of each other. Homes will become centers for connecting rather than boxes for holding.

In the past, homes were built as boxes on a grid system, for maximum efficiency with every person and family in their rightful place. While the box model might be best for a grid system, and perceived as the most efficient for furnishing, it is not the best energetic shape for connecting and living in harmony with nature. Some will choose to stay in their boxes for ease and convenience, until there comes a future when humanity outgrows their boxes entirely.

Homes of the future will have adequate acreage for family self-sufficiency, with each home being more circular to support a more natural family habitat. The family room, kitchen, and dining spaces will be at the center of the home where family and friends gravitate to connect and bond. Sleeping and working rooms extend off the main circular structure for continuous flow of energy from the power center, the heart of the home. Some may even choose to have circular or rounded edge furniture with no harsh angles. Furnishing will always be a personal preference, although the use of new plastics and harsh chemicals will no longer be considered a useful practice.

Each home will be self-sustaining and self-sufficient, producing its own power, collecting, and redistributing its own water, composting all waste, and repurposing whenever and wherever possible. Cleaned, and redistributed water will be used to water grass, gardens, and trees, and for distribution throughout houses for all use other than for drinking. Eventually, water will be so clean and plentiful you will no longer need your filtration and collecting methods and devices. Well water, spring water, and beautiful water fountains will continually oxygenate fresh water, pleasing eyes, ears, and pallets.

The mutual love and acceptance of all human beings working in harmony with the planet will open a window for the acceptance of otherworldly beings and star family, what you now commonly refer to as extraterrestrials, to make their physical appearance in the Earth realm. This will also include Earthlings being accepted into the Galactic Family and the Federation of Worlds. When the human family learns to be at peace with itself, it will be invited to play among the stars.

Home Models

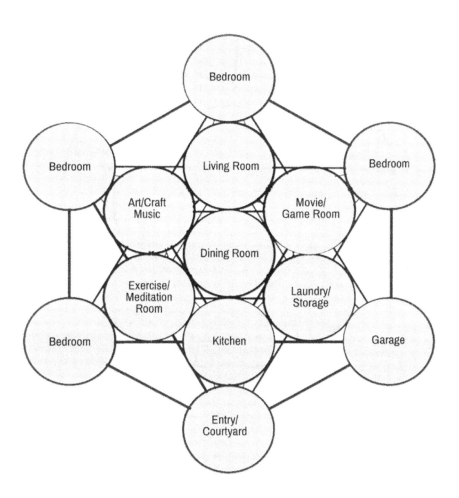

Bedroom

Bedroom

Bedroom

Living Room

Art/Craft
Music

Movie/
Game Room

Dining Room

Exercise/
Meditation
Room

Laundry/
Storage

Bedroom

Kitchen

Garage

Entry/
Courtyard

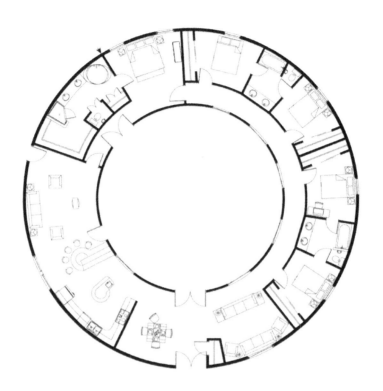

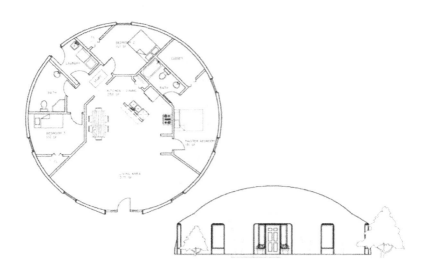

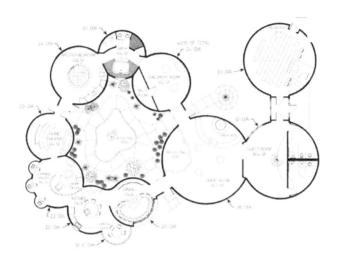

System 10. Spirituality

As with all other systems, your belief systems will also go through a metamorphosis as they evolve from fear-based dogma to true freedom of spirit and infinite connection to the Divine Love, Source Energy, Prime Creator many of you call God.

Religion and Spirituality

As you continue moving above and beyond fear you will begin to recognize the difference between religion and spirituality and choose the freedom of spirituality over the confines of religious dogma. Many of you are already pulling yourselves out of this control disguised as freedom and fear disguised as love found in many of your religiosities. As you ascend out of fear, judgment and division of any kind will disappear.

While much of humanity clings to their age-old beliefs handed down from generation upon generation, many of you are beginning to outgrow them as you search for more love and a direct connection to The One who is and creates all that is. As all your fear-based systems collapse or choose to evolve, religions and belief systems which cannot evolve to teach only love will eventually become another bygone concept in your collective human story.

All lifeforms are The Creator experiencing itself as life. All human beings are divinity having a human experience through each of you. In this knowing, a spiritual connection to oneself, the divine self within, is an integral part of the human experience. This coming home to the divine within is the search for home many of you have been seeking while not understanding it already exists within you. Heaven has always been within. Many of you are beginning to experience this for yourselves as you pull your minds and hearts out of the stories of fear.

Human beings will all eventually come to recognize that religions exist as a means for division and control. Their systems of belief cause a separation from one's own innate divinity and oneness with The Creator. Love is all that is and therefor you are all God, yet this concept has been difficult for many to grasp because their beliefs of separation created in fear have kept a stronghold on their minds and hearts. They set God outside themselves and as such experience a form of separation anxiety not understanding that separation is an illusion created in the minds of fear. When all human beings come home to God/Love in their own heart and let go of the division of "my way is the only way," all forms of religion will fade away into the spirit of love and what remains is a pure, limitless connection to The Divine. In that connection you will see all of life through the unconditional love and eyes of God through you.

Spiritual Centers

Churches and places of worship for an external God will become a thing of the past and be replaced with spiritual centers and gardens for direct connection with divine love and pure understanding. This connection stems from the human heart to all life on Earth, to the heart of Earth and beyond, and to the heart of The One Love of which all things are made.

Spiritual centers will be at the heart and core of every community along with other community services. They will be open for personal use, and loving guidance always. They are open to light and nature, rather than boxed in structures, with sliding walls of glass or crystal for protection from nature's elements when necessary. In these beautiful spaces dedicated to the spirit of love, all can commune with The Divine, in absolution of division and separation.

Until structured belief systems and long-held dogmas melt away, making way for higher understanding and connection with Source Creator, all beliefs will be equally supported and accepted. All-inclusive services may be a part of the spiritual center's spiritual growth opportunities, with no one minister or teacher at the helm. No one will be put on a pedestal and revered as better than. Teaching may be provided by a spiritual teacher feeling guided to teach, visiting teachers from other communities, and may often include multiple teachers in one session, with the understanding that all paths lead home to divine love within.

Spiritual ceremonies, such as the celebration of the birth of a child, a soul connection between beloveds, bridging ceremonies for life transitions, and celebrations of life for those who have left into the great beyond, are a welcome and joyful part of the Spiritual Center. Religious practices, specific to a particular system of belief, will be held elsewhere, as the spiritual center is the heart of all things non-partisan and will remain free of dogma, until dogma ceases to exist, and humanity all comes together in one heart. Eventually all religions will melt away as all humanity comes home to individual connection directly with Source and celebrates Divine Love in all things.

System 11. Technology

In many ways, Earth technology is only in its infancy. You have been using new technologies with ancient beliefs and wondering why not much has really changed. You've been repeating the same stories of war, over and over throughout your history, and wondering why you never arrive at lasting peace. You can never find peace through war and your war-torn hearts will always drive you into offense or defense. You build your technologies for war rather than for peace while peace for yourselves and your planet is what you desire most in your human experience.

As you update your beliefs and let go of fear, your technologies will improve to serve the best of all life, rather than being used to manipulate, oversee and destroy life. Weapons of war are yet another example of fear and control disguised of safety and security. When you look behind the veils and disguises, you will find the truth and liberate yourselves with the power of truth. You will be astounded by your technological advances hidden behind the veil of deception.

Technological Advancements

All life on Earth will experience the best of nature combined with nurture. New technologies will bring out the best possibilities for all. You will experience a renaissance of awareness as you revive ways of living and being which work in harmony with Earth while also experiencing a vast explosion of new technology which takes you into a whole new realm of understanding and experiencing your world. Your technologies reflect your consciousness. As you change your consciousness you will astound yourselves with what you will create.

You will liberate yourselves from all mechanisms intended to control you and experience advanced technologies which take you to the stars. Everything you can imagine in your mind's eye becomes possible and will no longer be hindered by beliefs and bureaucracy. You will all be free to imagine, design, build, create, perform, enhance, invent, and manifest new technologies which are only now just outside your reach. Many have already been invented and simply sit in offices and warehouses, waiting for all leashes and holds to be removed.

This is where the creative mind will thrive. This is where the minds and hearts of creatives merge with the technical and scientific minds and hearts, and you create concepts that were once only in your wildest dreams. Rather than competing, you will begin working together to create new concepts, techniques, and technologies. You will no longer create for profit or for the sake of governments and the military complex. There will only be the desire to create technologies in service to all life and the betterment of humanity.

You have so much to look forward to as you let go of everything that does not work and set your hearts and minds on what is possible. Humanity has only just begun its adventure into the universe of technological advancements. These will manifest in your reality once you are ready to use them only for love.

Personal Experiences

While some believe there will be a return to living off the Earth, scavenging for food as humanity did thousands of years ago, this will not be the case for most. This would indicate a total collapse of society and all progress made during your various ages of industry and growth. While the systems created in fear and greed will collapse, there will not be a collapse of society. This fall to dystopia is heralded in your movies yet it will not become your collective reality. Benevolent forces across the universe are at your side, working to assist you through this time of great transition.

There will be no scarcity, and no one will go hungry in your recreated world. Food will become pure and readily available without depleting the Earth or toiling in fields simply to eat. You will step outside into your luscious gardens and thriving greenhouses to meet your nutrient needs. Fresh, clean water will pour from every faucet, river, and stream. You will live in harmony with animals rather than feeling drawn to kill and eat them. Fear, scarcity, and mere survival will no longer exist for any being.

New technologies for healing and regenerating your bodies will be unleashed and improved upon. The original human design will come back online, resetting your full gene codex, expanding your capabilities, and extending your lives. This will help to ensure you enjoy the physicality of being human. You will experience new forms of travel which take you to places you've only ever imagined at seemingly impossible speeds.

All this you have within your reach and will manifest when enough of you change your hearts from fear to love. Your minds will be opened to the secrets of the cosmos and all your wildest dreams becomes realities.

System 12. Energy

Energy has never been meant for control as each person, and all living things, are a source of their own energy. Energy is intended to be freely given and received. It is a gift from the Earth and a resource from the heavens.

Harnessing Energy

It has long been known in your concept of reality that he who controls the power, controls the world. Energy is power and energy is in all things. It is time to reconsider how energy is harnessed, created, used, and controlled. It is time for the people to take back their power and receive what is rightfully theirs. Energy was always meant to be free and generously power every aspect of your world.

All those who have attempted to exploit and control energy as a source of their own power for the purpose of greed will have this power stripped from them as energy becomes freely given to all people. In your new world, every building, structure, occupation, and transportation will be provided with limitless, free, and clean energy.

Humanity will begin to access and utilize energy in ways energy has never been applied before. It will come from the stars, from the ethers, extracting invisible light from the darkness. Some of you are now recognizing this freely available energy, referring to it as scalar or quantum energy. Already there are those among you working with this energy and determining the best techniques and devices to capture and use it in your healing and technological modalities.

As the secrets of energy are unleashed and understood, humanity will first begin by harnessing this free-flowing energy through utilizing existing electrical structures and connections, to power their homes, streets, buildings and businesses. These modes for moving energy and power will be removed from the controls of corporations and given to the people through co-ownership and cooperation. Eventually, those old delivery systems will disappear as power lines, grid systems and electrical wires become obsolete, and every structure becomes the source of its own energy. Every home, business, building and construct will be fully self-sufficient and self-sustaining.

Powered by Nature

New technologies already in existence, yet hidden from the Earth realm, will begin to show themselves through human innovation. Never again will humanity be left in physical or metaphorical darkness. Yet you will not be left with artificial light. This new, more natural light will no longer block out the stars at night and human beings will no longer fear venturing out where they cannot see. The stars and celestial bodies will shine so bright there will be no need to light up every street and corner. There will be no reason to fear the nighttime air as it hums with its own light.

New innovations will be powered by nature. Not through utilizing or stretching natural resources, but through the air itself. As the air is cleaned of toxins and impurities, it becomes electric, and everything needed to power your innovations will be powered simply as they are. Every device will have a built-in receiver and generator. There will be no need for miles of wires or connecting to a grid. Energy is everywhere and it will be obtained by everything. You will never again need to concern yourselves with toxic waste and wasting the Earth's precious resources.

Waste-less

Human beings will come to a time of want-less and waste-less. The continual desire for consumption of the Earth and her resources will be replaced with a desire to preserve what already exists and restore what was taken. New technologies for de-energizing old waste will be created to ensure the Earth is no longer held captive to the continual cycle of consumption and waste and rather, all life will live in harmony with the cycle of creation, growth, utilization, end-of-use, and composition. Nothing will be wasted, only de-energized and energized into something entirely new.

Yes, you have already begun learning the lessons of recycling and recomposing. In this next energy revolution, you will make a new turn and you will learn how nothing goes to waste. These innovations will not go toward big profits of big companies who boast about how much they care while hiding how much they make. Those days of energy companies pillaging the planet while pretending to go green are over. These energy advances will benefit the people and the planet as nothing exists that cannot be de-energized and reenergized.

Eventually you will come to a time when all things are simply energized without draining one resource from the Earth as you come to see how all things are merely particles of energy bound in unique fashions. You will then simply choose what you desire, and it will be manifested from thin air as they say. But your air will not be thin. Instead, it will be thick with vibrant energy you may freely harness and utilize at will. This is when money will become inconsequential as all needs will be met simply for your own choosing. Your technologies will replicate everything you desire through pure energy.

This of course is in the distant future. Until then, you will need to learn to work together to better utilize your existing systems and services of support. Whenever and wherever possible try to live your life in the way of "do no harm." This is more than a reduction of carbon footprint, as has been labelled by those who have made money from this narrative. Rather, it is always being in full consciousness of how every choice affects your body, the body of others, and the body of Earth. When this becomes your focus, every choice you make begins to shift the entire human experience. Your world will become energized by the limitless energy and power of love.

Energy Sufficient

Harnessing the existing sources of power within your present realm of understanding includes recycling your own water, only heating or cooling rooms that need heating and cooling, and utilizing alternative energy sources such as wind, water, and sun. Using what you already know and have, you will focus on each home and business becoming fully self-sufficient rather than relying on municipalities and mega-corporations to provide your energy needs. Some may even find ways to share their resources with each other rather than giving energy to municipalities for selling to customers.

This requires thinking outside the boxes that have been carefully crafted to keep humanity under the overreaching power of corporations which exist for the sole purpose of profiting from fear. There is nothing to fear and there is no lack except for the perceived lack of ingenuity. Human beings are ingenious and have the capacity to shift every system to serve the greatest good. You need only find faith in yourselves rather than putting your faith in those who you have consciously and unconsciously chosen to have power over you.

All the energy you need to run a free and clear world is at your fingertips and it only requires a willingness to see outside the box of what presently is and begin creating from your inventive minds. There is no lack, and resources are not running thin. This is yet another narrative created in fear by those who wish to control you. The only lack is lack of faith in yourselves and your own power. Energy is everywhere, it is limitless and abundant, and you will learn how to harness it in a whole new way.

Your Energy

Undoubtedly, you've heard the saying that time is energy and energy is money. This is simply not true. The concept of time and using time for money was created as a concept to control your personal energy. In the near distant future, your concept of time will shift, and you will no longer run your lives by a mechanical concept of time.

You will learn to follow the rhythm of your bodies and trust in divine timing. You will learn to balance being with doing while being your loving essence and doing what you love. You will no longer be driven, driving your minds, hearts, and bodies into disease and exhaustion while chasing the illusion of financial prosperity through hard work. Rather, you will all come to understand that prosperity is your very essence, and you will all work in harmony to ensure your collective prosperity and the prospering of your collective home. Your planet contains everything you all need to thrive and prosper, you need only to respect and honor her, and she will open her greatest assets to you. There is much you have yet to learn about her capabilities and your symbiotic relationship with her.

You will learn to guard your personal energy as the essence of who you are and share it openly and freely with those who resonate at your same frequency. You will no longer give your energy away to engross the pocketbooks of others as you learn to attune to your own energetic frequency. Your energy, your frequency, in perfect harmony will become the utmost priority. You will come to understand how your energy and the frequency you carry within your whole being of mind, body, heart, and spirit, becomes the energy and frequency of everything around you.

Your very resonance is what powers you. As you come to fully understand this and that you are one with all that is, your personal energy will become your primary focus. Knowing that your energy is always reflected back to you, you will come to fully understand that as you give you also receive. You will appreciate how this cycle of energy, emitted from your hearts, powers all things.

System 13. Entertainment

Even in times when resources have appeared to be scarce and experiences at their worst, human beings have always found a way to be entertained. You gather in your community centers, churches, theaters, parks, playhouses, and homes for the pure purpose of entertainment. Entertainment allows you to live in your imagination and escape your reality. In a sense, being entertained permits you to be out of your minds.

Response to Fear

Long ago it was discovered that entertaining people through fear was an excellent device for control. Over the millennia this was perfected with very few humans becoming aware of these tactics of manipulation through fear disguised as entertainment. As fear became more subtle and more entertaining it also became more effective. Gone are the days of lions eating humans for entertainment and gladiators fighting for their lives, but your modern-day entertainment and your official news, with its violence and death still creates the same internal response to stress. A mind in fear is easier to control.

Modern entertainment employs techniques utilized though the careful study of marketing, psychology, and human response. Vast funds have been invested in understanding what makes the human mind work and how to manipulate it to illicit a particular reaction. These ploys have been used across the board from your pulpits and theaters to television and social media. Almost all of it is created with intent to hold humanity in fear and division.

In a reality based in fear, all news, programming, stories, and entertainment continually promote fear-based narratives. The human stories, from the beginning of known time, primarily tell of drama and trauma, wars and pestilence, violence, and starvation. These fear-based narratives have humanity stuck in the cycle of fear and blindly believing this is the only way. Entire industries have been created to keep humanity enslaved by fear.

Human beings believe what they see and what they believe then creates reality. This creation through visualization is one way the human design is so extraordinary and powerful.

Those who serve the dark side of the contrast are aware of the power of the human mind to create what it envisions, even when the visioning is unconscious. They know that by feeding humanity dystopian visions, humanity unknowingly creates the very thing they fear. Television became the greatest tool for telling visions the dark side of the contrast wishes for humanity to create through the power of your minds. It is used for programming the human mind in the disguise of harmless entertainment programs.

Know Dear Ones, that time is rapidly coming to an end. All people, corporations and technologies which promote fear will become extinct. They will be pulled from their positions and posts and stripped of their titles and assets. Enough of you have become aware of their manipulation tactics and are no longer willing to support their schemes. You have chosen to be free from fear and the universe has listened.

The technologies created to hold you in fear and darkness are being repurposed on behalf of love and light. As all the constructs of fear are imploded, some technologies will remain and be upgraded to serve a higher purpose. Among these are your sources of entertainment. You will be given new visions to envision and new stories to establish a new reality through. Your minds will be given new possibilities and programs to run. You will start changing your world without many of you even being conscious of how thoughts create reality.

New Stories

Some may argue that eutopia isn't possible. That is only because dystopia is all humanity has ever been shown. Although there have been glimpses of bliss, the overarching narrative has been that happiness never lasts. That is an old narrative and in your new world, happily ever after does exist. You need only believe it and begin creating it for yourselves.

The delicate and easily permeable human mind believes what it is told and creates reality based on what it is programmed with. Social programming creates entire cultures and beliefs. Knowing this, humanity can begin telling new stories of what is possible and what has been. You will create new social programming of hope, real love, mutual support, human potential, and infinite possibilities. When you stop telling stories of war and violence, war and violence will cease. When you start only telling stories of love and potential, this will become the new collective reality.

This new programming with stories of resilience, inspiration, creation, and potential will move humanity out of the fear-based reality and into infinite possibilities. You will see beyond the old stories of pain and suffering and learn the truth of your brilliance. All pain and drama can become nothing more than learning lessons from the past when people are taught how to see beyond it. Any stories of suffering will only be used for teaching what is possible in a way that is genuinely entertaining and internally transforming. Human beings crave inspiration, and they will be fed what they crave most. Inspiration through entertainment will drive an entirely new reality.

Conscious Media

The concept of an entertainment "industry" will be replaced with the understanding of how entertainment is a service. It serves to enlighten the human mind to its fullest capabilities. It serves to teach a new model of the human story – the true story. It serves to educate possibilities, and it serves to create a new vision for humanity.

New conscious entertainment and media are emerging and will ensure all beings are fed only the loving truth of what has been, what is, and what can be. Movies, television shows, podcasts, music, games, and books based only on love will overtake all airwaves, shelves, and hand-held devices. Love will stream through every theater, living room and apparatus. History will be shown through the eyes of understanding, acceptance, and forgiveness of the past, with lessons extracted for how to no longer live in fear. True stories will show what is possible and humanity will be inspired to rise to its own occasion.

Television will begin telling new visions of love, hope, dignity, and faith. The new news will tell the whole truth and will share stories of love rather than fear, the goodness of humanity rather than doom and gloom. New channels will focus on possibilities rather than atrocities and nonfiction will focus on harmony rather than war. The story arc will shift to include resolution and completion of the story cycle where the hero becomes the teacher and will change from a focus on conflict to focusing on the transformation.

Humanity, although assumed to be addicted to fear and conflict, won't even miss the violence once it is gone. The human heart craves inspiration, and the mind craves possibilities above all else. Human beings have always loved the hero story because it ignites the hero and heroine within all of you. People will be too busy being entertained by what is real and inspiring, what makes them celebrate life, they won't even look for stories of fear, violence, and suffering.

As human beings are reminded of who they really are, you will see a new form of entertainment that not only delights the mind, but it also causes an internal shift of consciousness and understanding. They might not know it yet because human beings have been fed a continual diet of fear, but they will come to see that death and violence in storytelling is not necessary to create a transformational story or to bond with characters in the story. The real conflict is inner conflict and that is what makes a character and the story most memorable. The hero's and heroine's journey will shift from scenes of suffering and violence to the more real depiction of the inner journey of self-discovery and transcendence.

Stories of history will focus on the courage and ingenuity of humanity rather than wars and violence. As humanity learns its collective lessons from the past, the past will no longer repeat itself. Human beings have been so busy beating the drums of their past sufferings, they have unknowingly kept themselves in the continual state of victimization and oppression. You will all come to see the past as nothing more than collective lessons to learn from and recognize the past as a reference of "how humans used to live and behave," and you will be grateful you no longer live that way. You will carve a new human story, highlighting the hearts and geniuses of the past, and thus, the belief in humanity and your limitless capabilities will become the beliefs of all. Learning through entertainment speeds that process.

The new world you create from the ashes of the old world of fear labeled as entertainment will be so much richer than anything you've ever seen on your viewing devices and platforms. You will find yourselves seeking out entertainment and experiences which inspire you to reach to new heights within yourselves.

In this loving reality you will all begin to grasp your oneness and will have no desire to cause harm in any way. As you move forward and let go of all attachments to the stories of your past, your descendants will look back in puzzlement at how things used to be when fear ruled the world.

THE
SOLUTIONS

Section 3
THE SOLUTIONS

The truth that love heals and creates all things will become the face of all human beliefs and practices and be behind all concepts and models. Where do each of you begin in the creation of these new concepts and models? Begin with feeling through your hearts rather than thinking with your minds. Allow your worried minds to quite the voices of fear, worry and doubt. This is the old, stale energy attempting to stifle your limitless connection to your own mind of creation, and the mind of Source.

You are all creators, made in the likeness of The One Love which is and creates all things. There has never been a separation between you and Source Creator. Your ability to create as master creators on behalf of and in cooperation with The One has always been present in your reality. You are all aspects of The Divine experiencing itself as each of you. As such, you are already master creators and need only find your infinite capacities within yourselves. When you breath into your heart and open it up to create in alignment with the heart of Source, you will astound yourselves.

Source, the Infinite Allness many call God, is both Mother and Father, masculine and feminine. As such, we refer to Source as It or Them, rather than Him or Her, He or She. Understand this is not the same as your present gender conversations as this is yet another example of the inversion on your present playing field. We speak of energy rather than form. The One does not limit itself to form. It is all that is, and all that is, is made of Its infinite loving essence. Love is and creates all things.

For far too long Humanity has ignored its Mother, and in so doing, experienced a collective separation anxiety and limited your ability to create in Her image. As you connect your hearts with the heart of Mother Creator and Mother Earth, you will feel love and compassion for all beings in a way never felt before in your known human story. Here you will find the love necessary to recreate your world in a way that serves all beings everywhere.

When your minds attune to the Divine Masculine mind and your hearts attune to the Divine Feminine heart, you become and unstoppable force for creation. This is about the reunification of your whole being as your hearts are healed to work to their fullest and greatest capacity. In this unification and rebalancing of Divine Masculine and Divine Feminine in each of your minds and hearts, everything becomes possible. All things both masculine and feminine already exist within you, it is only a matter of recognizing both and utilizing them to their fullest potential as The One Divine Love works through you and as you.

Begin with choosing which issues and/or systems you feel calling to your heart. The new reality you are building is heart-based rather than a mental construct. Being out of your egoic mind is the beginning of creating with your imagination, your heart, and your connection to the infinite intelligence and wisdom of Source. Imagination creates reality and you could not even imagine unless the potential for creation didn't already exist. You need to trust this truth and begin creating with this knowledge.

You are all the divine children and creators made in the image of Source Creator. You need only trust your own brilliance, the brilliance of others and work in cooperation with your combined brilliance. Move your mind out of the old question of "what's in it for me" and flip it into the heart-centered question of "what is best for we?" When you shift your focus from me to we, you will begin to see the limitless possibilities and you will begin to create your new world in a way that almost feels like magic.

Solution 1. Rethink Education

It is time for humanity to rethink education and reconstruct it from the ground up. This rethinking of education begins within your own homes and communities, rather than feeling compelled to recreate entire systems. Remember, the systems were created to control thinking rather than expanding your minds.

Until the controls over education are dismantled, and constructs of the old world dissolved, opening new education models under the umbrella of a private association may be necessary in some communities. Private associations allow for each member to become an integral part of how the school is structured, developed, and managed. Every parent is a valued voting member, along with every teacher and counselor. Children are also invited to provide input on how they can best be served.

Decisions are made by group consensus rather than by a school board with one person at the top. Parents may take turns leading the meetings, thus ensuring no one person holds a continual leadership position. This cooperative leadership model may stretch the imagination, and it is where humanity is heading. A private membership learning center allows parents and teachers to guide children's learning outside of the systemized instruction model, and free from all governmental and religious constructs. Small schools, particularly at the elementary level, allow for smaller classrooms and more customized teaching for each student.

Within your communities, begin gathering with parents who want more for their children and with teachers who desire to use their creativity and love of children to teach outside of the existing constraints and who agree with this new model of learning. There are many at this time of great change who are no longer willing to wait for those who are in existing positions of leadership to make changes on the people's behalf. There are too many individuals, organizations, and corporations which have their fingers in the proverbial pot of education for any real changes to be made from within your present systems. Changes will only come when enough parents use their own resources and remove their children from existing establishments. Changes to the system will come then system establishments feel the financial sting.

Well-informed parents who have done their research and know their children deserve better than the status quo will choose to take their children elsewhere. When enough parents bond together on behalf of their children, and create child-centered curriculums, the systems will shift to follow suit.

Seek out teachers and other parents in your community. Start a private association education center or set up a learning pod. Work together on the curriculum and services which support the needs of all students, parents, and teachers. When enough of you do this taking of matters into your own hands, it will become your new normal. As a community of parents, caregivers, and teachers, you have the power within you to create your own unique learning environments.

Gather with other parents and teachers, in a desire to create a better way of educating children, and heart-storm with your ideas and a plan for unity. Combine your concerns, desires, and insights. Pool your resources and resourcefulness. Create a concept that best serves the parents, teachers, and children in your given group. This may be a home-school where one parent oversees the education of several families while other parents go to work and assist by paying the educating parent to care for and educate their children. Perhaps it is a learning pod where parents take turns hosting the children, each on a given day of the week. Or it may be that many of you decide to band together your resources and hire a teacher to oversee the education of your children in a small group setting. These learning environments work well for both parents and students without pressure on any one individual family.

For others, this may mean starting your own private membership education facility, with multiple teachers and subjects to create a more school-like setting for social as well as educational purposes. Consider this as a private school but with less rigid programming and free of indoctrination. There is no one-right-way, only the way that works best for you and those in your circles of care.

Solution 2. Focus on Wellbeing

Begin by connecting with healthcare and wellness providers to determine how satisfied they are with the existing structures. Many in the medical field are disenchanted with the system and wish to expand beyond the constraints placed on them by "the industry." The medical industry is presently mandated and controlled by government structures, insurance companies, and chemical industries and prohibits genuinely caring healthcare practitioners from providing the health and wellness they studied in their years of education. Many desire the freedom to practice as they choose and expand into new fields currently limited by their agreements to the system.

Gather like-minded healthcare and wellness practitioners and begin creating new concepts for private wellness centers. Within a member format, healthcare practitioners are not limited to doing business in the traditional way. As one cohesive team, practitioners can coordinate, cooperate, and collaborate in unique processes that serve to heal the whole being of their clients and patients, beyond just bandaging symptoms with pharmaceutical protocols and insurance regulations.

Being of service and caring for patients and clients must take precedence over making money while also knowing your personal needs are being met. When enough medical personnel liberate themselves from the system and begin creating their own protocols and mutually supporting services, patients will be healed of their disease with greater ease. Patients will begin to seek out these healing protocols before medicating with traditional medicine. This will then become the new face of medicine and wellness as external systems shift to meet and serve the true needs of people.

Solution 3. Replenish the Environment

Choose to no longer wait for government programs, which only desire to raise taxes and move people from the countryside into cities where human beings are more easily manageable. Rather, take matters into your own hands. Gather with others in your communities and create real solutions to all the issues facing your community. Whether it be your local community or the global community, begin by envisioning the actions necessary to make the changes you want to see occur, then move forward in divinely guided action.

There is no need to wait for anyone else to start the initiatives and gather resources. Each of you have within you the initiative to change everything in the world around you. Have tree planting parties. Start butterfly gardens. Maintain honeybee hives. Plant water-soluble grass. Grow herbs. Start community gardens. Work from home. Walk rather than drive when possible. Eat fresh and organic and eat less. Support your farmer's markets and local farms. Choose foods that are not factory packaged adds to the landfills. Research where your food, clothing and personal products are sourced and produced. Watch how your personal choices leave an imprint on the body of Earth.

Use the ingenuity of your minds and the compassion of your hearts to create new concepts not yet created for cleaning, clearing, and replenishing the Earth. Everything you can imagine already exists in the ethers, and only requires your genius to bring it from imagination into formation.

You may also choose to participate in class-action lawsuits to hold corporations, bureaucrats, and billionaires accountable for the mess they have made and demand climate justice on behalf of the Earth herself. Stay out of hatred and blame while also expecting their accountability. Hold them to their words of wanting to make the world a better place and put their money behind their words. Choose to no longer be shy about the power you have as individuals banding together as one voice on behalf of all life on Earth. As her caregivers you are also her protectors. As Earth's protectors it is up to you to stand up on her behalf and make the changes necessary for all of you to thrive.

Solution 4. Grow Better Agriculture

Food and water are the most basic of all human needs and need to be tended to with sacredness and loving care. Begin by learning how to grow your own food, even if it's a few small herbs in the window or pots on your patio. This begins connecting your heart to nature and to the heart of your Earth mother.

Grow an appreciation for Earth Science and the web of life. Support local farmers and small grocers over conglomerate chains where produce is picked early and often spends weeks in the transportation process, losing much of its nutritional content and is often artificially ripened in chemical processes. Shop local, support local, thrive local.

Start community gardens in empty plots of land. You may need to petition your local municipality or ask for volunteered lots. Create on-site composting to ensure the land is continually replete with nutrients. Remember, all plants pull carbon from the air and into the Earth where it regenerates the soil. Let plants compost into the soil after each growing season and watch the miracle of nature unfold. Read up on which weeds to leave because they are edible and helpful, and which ones to remove. Learn about which flowers are edible, help to attract insect helpers, and deter disease, and which ones attract unhelpful bugs and spread disease. Discover which plants mutually support each other in your growing environment and grow your gardens as nature intended.

Meet with others in your community who see the value of growing food rather than hunting for it at food-chains, then merge your creative geniuses into mutual ideas Each person has their own ingenuity and together you can create concepts which have never been seen before. Think with your hearts rather than with your heads and you will begin to see what is possible when you work together on behalf of all of you.

Community gardens, private in the beginning until the dust settles, will become the normal way humanity will be fed and nourished, eventually weaning themselves from artificially packaged and chemically induced foods. This is not to say that preserving food will become a thing of the past, only that a more natural preservation process will take its place. Every person will begin to see the value in eating food as close to the source as possible. Restaurants may also choose to participate in a co-op garden and ranch, or have their own garden, serving only fresh, natural ingredients to their customers. The more people demand fresh, local and organic, the more you will see businesses spring into action to meet the desires of the people.

Solution 5. Replace Governance

When you discover your own ability to self-regulate through love you will all see how external governance really isn't necessary. All people who live in love from the inside out do not need anyone else telling them how to live their lives. They know their lives are a magnificent presence on the planet and live in service to love in all things. Every choice they make stems from the heart of love for themselves and for all life. This is the new face of leadership as individuals learn how to self-direct and self-govern.

Begin by recognizing that each of you are born leaders and each of you has greatness within. Each person has the capacity to lead their own lives and be a way-shower for others to lead their own lives. Leaders teach other leaders how to lead. Leadership from the heart simply says, "follow my lead" rather than, "follow me." When you understand the difference, you will get out of ego's way and lead from the heart of hearts.

Gather with others who see a new possibility and create leadership pods where you work cohesively to create new concepts for your communities. Then take what you have learned and spread it outward across the airwaves so that others may learn how to duplicate what you've created and begin using it in their own communities. Share ideas and possibilities until they become viral and overtake all old leadership models.

Remember, true leadership does not place one above another, it reinforces that every person's voice and perspective has value and incorporates a vision that works for everyone. Creating leadership pods where chosen voices from each concept meet and converge ideas, rather than one person at the top controlling all others, will rapidly shift everything in your communities.

Those who choose to take on leadership roles need understand their role as a guide and core member, rather than superior. Create programs where the leadership roles change frequently to prevent any one person from having too much power or becoming overburdened. In your businesses, associations, and communities, redesign your leadership models from the inside out rather than from the top down, and you will begin to see how everyone thrives and feels supported.

Solution 6. Create New Economics

First, you must understand that money is not evil, nor does it create evil beings. It is simply a tool created of Earth's goodness in support of her beings and can be used either for control or for transformation. How it is used stems from the size of the heart using it and lust for it creates greed. Your present concept of money is a tool for wielding the change you seek. It will continue to be a tool for the transformation you desire until it is no longer a part of your collective experience. When you begin merging money with love, it will transform your world.

Begin by remembering that you have the power of choice and by understanding that your present economic systems serve no one except those who run the systems. Once you accept this, you can begin to change it. Remember, all purchasing power is in the hands of people and you make your wishes known by letting your money speak for you. Those who run the money systems are aware of your power to transform entire economies by the decisions you make. They invest untold sums on marketing and campaigns to drive your choices. You each choose, whether those choices are conscious or not, whether to buy into their campaigns and what they sell you. Understand Dear Ones, every penny they invest in drawing you into their agenda is a penny they've invested in themselves.

You choose which businesses thrive and which businesses fail by where you choose to spend your money. Choose to no longer support corporate empires and instead support your local communities and independent businesses. Choose to support and empower each other rather than those who do not care about you and to whom you are nothing more than money in their pocketbooks. Choose to invest in each other's businesses rather than the stock market which is based on greed and manipulation. Choose to experience the convenience of meeting your local business owners and supporting them, rather than sending your money elsewhere and wait for products and services to show up at your door. Choose to know your neighbors, who they are and what they do for a living. Learn how you can mutually support each other's endeavors.

Rather than squandering your money on needless things, be selective. Choose companies, products and services which serve a greater purpose beyond making money. Do your research to ensure who they are and what they stand for. Local companies which haven't gained notoriety or sold out on the public arena are more likely to provide better service and higher quality goods.In the beginning it may be more expensive, but only until "shopping local" becomes your normal practice, and the massive uncaring corporations can no longer compete with the hearts of homespun and mutually supported businesses.

If you are a business owner, begin by pulling yourself out of the economic systems and regulations as much as possible. This becomes feasible through membership-based associations. These are interim business concepts until taxes and government regulations no longer interfere with personal prosperity. Running a private business allows you to run your business your way and treat your customers with the dignity and respect they deserve without government overreach standing in the way of who, how, when, and where you can do business.

Solution 7. Let Go of Defense

Rather than trying to figure out how you can buy more weapons of defense, as many presently do, focus instead on how you can mutually support each other and create an environment where defense is no longer necessary. Take the ball in your court and go on the offense. This is where your true power lies.

Gather with others in your community who wish to know longer tolerate tyranny and vote for a reduction in policing by force. Work together to hold those who appear to have power over you to their own commitment of support and protect. Demand those you have chosen to lead to hold to their word as servants of the people. Stand up to those who demand you fight each other and refuse to fight. When enough people stop seeing each other as the enemy, all attempts to control people through force and fear will no longer be effective. It is simply impossible to enforce war when no one is willing to fight.

Remember the stories of the great leaders who lead by peace instead of war. They are remembered as peace makers and not warriors, and for that, their names and legacies stand the test of time. See this peace for yourselves and for all life on Earth and be willing to be among the peace makers. Choose to put down your weapons and take up arms with each other, remembering that you are all one family and together you will create a new world where war and hate are bygone thoughts.

Solution 8. Consciously Develop

For much of your human story, your developments were created by those who owned the land and developed in accordance with their plans for overseeing the people. While this has not always been the case, for much of your known time landowners had more freedom than those who worked the land on the landowner's behalf. Even now, many of you have the illusion of owning your own land. You pay money to the banks which own the title and taxes to the municipalities which work in contract with the lending institutions. You appeal to your overseers for the right to build on the property you have the illusion of owning. All of that will change as your economic systems fail and are reconstructed as service. People, rather than institutions, will own the land and you will rework your developments in service to love.

Begin by envisioning how your developments will appear. Which buildings need to disappear and what will replace them when they are gone? If you choose to stay in your existing community, what do you envision staying and going? Do you see business buildings being imploded and the empty space used for green space, or do you see corporate buildings being restructured for living spaces? When enough of you envision a thing, it will be done. If you feel guided to move to a private, sustainable community, what does that look like for you? What do you want your living environment to look and feel like? Remember, your vision creates your reality.

Gather with others who have similar concepts, and pool your ideas, visions, and resources. If leadership roles call to you, choose to volunteer in community leadership. When enough of you band together in unity and purpose, you can change your existing communities to serve the greatest purpose in support of all. For example, if enough of you become members of your local school board, you may be able to change how the school is managed or if enough of you choose to participate in your city councils, you will change how your city is managed. This of course is until these leadership models are no longer necessary.

If you choose an intentional community, reach out across the airwaves and either find an existing intentional community which resonates with your heart or gather with other like minds to pool your resources and ideas to begin your own community. Remember, all things are possible through vision and unification.

Solution 9. Expand Relationships

When you begin to understand that family extends beyond your birth family and bloodline, you can see that family is everywhere. As you let go of those who no longer resonate with you because they cannot see what you see, your soul family will begin to emerge on your path. You will build new relationships based on unconditional love, mutual support, and genuine acceptance.

Begin by letting go of your attachments to how you believe your partner's paths, children's paths, and the paths of others should look like. Your own suffering stems from your attachments to your programming of how things should be. When you let go of attachments, and begin seeing your beloveds as energetic connections, you will recognize who and what to let go of and who to keep by your side. You will begin to also recognize soul family and develop new loving relationships as false friendships slip away.

In this new awareness, you will gain a deeper appreciation and gratitude for those in your life as you no longer fear them fading from your life or onto a path that does not fit into your belief of who they need be. You will begin to see those nearest you as soul family with a connection often deeper and more meaningful that those of blood relatives. This extended family of loving support will help you redefine your relationships with immediate family as you learn to let go of what no longer serves you or them and make choices which are best for all concerned.

You may find old family slipping away as new family gravitates toward you, and you will have a renewed appreciation for your human family of origin, even if you choose to let them go on their own journey away from you.

Solution 10. Grow Spiritually

Every issue in your human experience is ultimately a spiritual issue. The emptiness felt by so many of you stems from a disconnection and misunderstanding of your true divine nature. When you go inside your own being, rather that look outside for answers, you will find the connection to truth. When you grow the light in your hearts, all disease and suffering will go by the wayside. You will find peace on Earth within yourselves.

Begin by understanding the difference between religion and spirituality and choose love-based beliefs over fear-based dogma. This doesn't mean you need to abandon your religions, only that you consciously choose which beliefs to help guide you forward and which beliefs no longer serve your soul's purpose through you. If there is a fear attached to any belief, recognize that it is fear-based deception, and not from the heart of divine love. Recognize your direct connection to The Divine, the Source of all that is, by whatever name or label you choose. Each of you has the capacity to commune directly with The One, as you are all already one with it. You need only let go of all beliefs of separation and the systems set up to keep you separate from each other and from Source.

You are all emanations of The Divine. The recognition that you are Divine Spirit having a human experience will then gravitate you toward others who recognize this for themselves. In this understanding and enlightened awareness, memberships and organizations that were once created for the containment of the human spirit are no longer necessary. You may choose to follow a spiritual master or masters who resonate with your own soul and will no longer resonate with a particular system of belief.

This is the new face of spiritual community. It is not a physical community, but rather a communication and communion of spirit. Your spiritual communities may meet in green spaces, beautiful buildings, or across the airwaves. How you meet matters not, as energy transcends all physical forms. Communion of hearts is all that is necessary.

As you gravitate away from systemized religions and into the universality of oneness, Divine Love experiencing itself as each of you, you will no longer feel the division and separation now tugging at your hearts. You will transcend fear as you come to understand that fear itself is an illusion and Love really is all that is. As you learn to fully embody Divine Love, you will create the heaven on Earth now seeking to be birthed through each of you.

Solution 11. Embrace Technology

Many of you are aware of and fear the narrative pushing humanity toward transhumanism in the promise of everlasting life. Know this Dear Ones, in the reality you are seeking to create, you will not be merged with artificial intelligence. Eternal life through artificial integration is a lie fed to humanity as the next phase in your collective evolution. The dark side of the contrast is a mirror image of the light side, and many cannot differentiate between what is real and what is the mirror image. The mirror image is an illusion attempting to make itself real and flip the mirror and overtake the side of light.

Remember Dear Ones, there is a vast difference between the external push for transhumanism and internal pull toward transformation. These are opposite ends of the human evolution spectrum. Transhumanism is driven by technology for artificial life while transformation is organic and restores the true Divine Human to your fullest potential. Some may choose to artificially inseminate themselves with inorganic materials in the promise of living forever, and as they do, they lose their connection to The Divine which streams through the hearts of all organic beings.

Those who choose transformation and the recreation of your world through love will see how to use technology for the advancement of all life, rather than the manipulation of life, and work with the Source Creator which creates through each of you. The genius of the human mind in co-creation with the mind of Source/God makes all things possible. When your visions are sparked to life and fed love from your hearts, you will transform your world.

Begin with understanding that much of the technology you seek is already in existence and only needs to be unveiled and unwrapped. Everything you seek already exists and needs only to physically manifest. You wouldn't be able to imagine it if it didn't already exist energetically. It exists in the field of creation waiting to be dropped into your playing field. As you learn to trust yourselves rather than giving your trust to external sources, you will astound yourselves with what you are capable of.

Once the veil is lifted for humanity, these technologies will rapidly advance in your collective reality. Many physically existing technologies will be repurposed for positive effect as you restructure your world. The mechanisms which have been used to control your weather will be used to regenerate a green Earth. Techniques presently used for recovery and reverse aging in your secret government programs will be used to heal the masses. The technology used to control energy will be replaced with free and limitless energy. As your minds are restored to service over self-preservation you will also reprogram any artificial intelligence with this same focus. It will serve life rather than attempt to control life.

Those who are technically inclined will experience the joy of participating in this unfoldment and the creation of entirely new technologies given to you by those from above who will teach and assist you. You will experience an explosion of ideas and visions for what is possible as you move from fear to love. You are entering the Age of Ingenuity where you all work in cooperation with for the benefit and restoration of all life on Earth.

There is nothing you need to "do" other than embrace these new advancements meant for the betterment of humanity as they replace all technology meant for the control of all life on Earth. If you are technically or engineering-inclined, listen to your inner guidance to help you create what you envision and embrace the invitation to be on creation teams. This is where you will shine at your brightest as the future is all-hands-on-deck working through the inter-creation of your new world.

Solution 12. Understand Energy

As many of you are aware, everything in existence is energy. There are many waves of energy yet to be discovered and utilized in your human experience. All energies are derived from love as the force that is and creates all things. As the human mind evolves to understand its limitlessness you will see into the vastness of the energy field beyond the human eye. Simply put, although you cannot see love, you aware of its existence. The same holds true for all energy waves. As your minds evolve out from under the shroud of fear, you will learn to recognize and harness newfound energy presently outside of your conceptualization.

Begin by first learning to navigate and manage your own personal energy through higher vibration thoughts, foods, family, and friends. By letting go of what does not serve your own highest and greatest good, your energy is lifted, and you resonate at a more loving frequency. This then extends into the world around you and energizes everyone in your periphery. You are, in essence, your own living battery.

Regarding your home and immediate surroundings, begin by decluttering your personal space and letting go of anything attached to old energy. Let it go entirely or transmute it and infuse it with new loving energy. Creating an energetically clear space allows for new energy to move in and new options to be made available to you.

Powering your home or place of business begins with utilizing the present alternate sources for energizing your space. Use the sun, wind, and nature to power your life, rather than bleeding Earth of her oils and poisoning her ground, while you choose to live within the present energy grid. Energize your homes with fans, open windows, fresh air, and green plants. Think outside the box about using energy more wisely. These will be interim solutions until new energy technologies come online and you free yourselves of all attachments to the energy grid.

In all you do think kindness for the Earth as your mother, giver, and nurturer of life. As you create new concepts for improving, lighting, and energizing your world, think of her first and how your choices impact your mother. Let all you do be about love and reverence for the one from which all life comes, and all life returns to.

Solution 13. Enjoy Entertainment

The change you seek to create within your world begins within yourselves and your willingness to restructure your internal perspectives. So many of you wish to recreate your outer world without recreating your inner world. This is not how the creation process works. You cannot create a new reality within the confines of old beliefs. If you wish to create a love-based reality you must first expand love within yourselves.

Begin with processing your own story and telling it from a new perspective. All change begins within the individual. All collective transformation begins with personal transformation. Telling a better human story begins with each person telling their own pain story from a new loving perspective. If you are to have a better future, it begins with telling better stories about your past and present. Telling better stories about the past and present leads toward better stories of future possibilities.

As each person tells their story from a position of self-empowerment and learning from experience, rather than from a position of victimization and resentment, it will become how all stories are told. This new way of storytelling will eventually lead to peace within all beings and peace on Earth.

The more each human being tells their personal story from a more loving perspective, the more this concept of telling empowered stories will spread forward. This will also be applied to the collective human story which will liberate the entire human family from all constructs of fear. Humanity will no longer repeat the old story because all lessons will have been learned from the past and all stories moving forward will be based on possibilities and potential, rather than on suffering.

The story arc will shift from three parts with a focus on the internal and external conflict, to a four-part story focusing on the return and resolution of the hero. This coming home and healing the story is a necessary part of restructuring how human beings look at the human experience. It will help to make peace with your collective past and present and create more hope for the future.

If you are a creative, begin by seeking out other conscious creatives and seeing how you can mutually support each other and begin creating projects based on cooperation rather than looking to the over-bloated names and hierarchies presently found in the world of entertainment. Seek out new talent with a genuine love and heart for acting, dancing, singing, illustrating, and entertaining. Merge your creative ideas and talents into concepts which lift humanity, showing what is possible.

Create concepts showing the truth of what has been and with a focus on "this is how things used to be but not anymore." Create projects which genuinely entertain while also integrating learning through visceral experience. Create storylines and events as experiences where your audiences feel with their bodies rather than simply be entertained in their minds. Take your focus off entertainment as a means for generating money and recognize it for the priceless service it provides. Reach human beings at their hearts rather than their egos, and then watch the world transform right before your eyes.

The entertainment industry can change the world faster than any other modality. When enough of you understand this and choose to participate in creating and enjoying conscious entertainment rather than default programming, everything will change in an instant. Everything in your world will change when enough of you refuse to invest your time, energy, and money into anything that is not loving.

When you choose love, compassion and understanding and make that the core of every story you tell, your world will never be the same. As love becomes the basis of your new normal in all things, you will begin to forget what it was to live in fear.

RESOURCES

Resources

As humanity heads into the unknown world. It is vital that all those who can see the greater picture now focus on what is possible for humanity even as you face your collective breaking down and the suffering may feel intolerable. As humanity moves through its collective dark night of the soul and processes its shadows, it is vital you hold yourselves in the pure, divine, unconditional love of Divine Oneness. You've now seen what is possible on the other side of the bridge as together you restructure your world.

Upon completion of the information given to me by Metatron, I took it upon myself to search for resources I feel will be helpful to you to get you started in the role you feel calling to you. Every person plays a vital role in the creation of our new reality and one person really can make a difference. For a continually expanding list of solutions and resources visit: RecreatingEarth.Earth.

Adult Education and Membership

- https://wethepeoplepmapower.com/
- https://thefreedompeople.org/services/pma
- https://livefree.academy/

New Earth Projects

- https://transcendthematrix.com/projects/humanitarian-project-submissions/
- https://newEarthproject.org/wp-content/assets/docs/ne_blueprint.pdf
- https://www.edenproject.com/
- https://newearthcooking.com/team-new-earth/

Health and Wellness

- https://www.lifestylemedicine.com/

Domes, Homes, and Construction

- https://www.solardome.co.uk/education/schools/
- https://monolithicdome.com/
- https://pacificdomes.com/
- https://www.biodomes.eu/
- https://vikingdome.com
- https://www.dwell.com/article/geodesic-dome-homes-2ea4ca66

- https://inhabitat.com/5-great-reasons-to-build-a-geodesic-dome-home/dome/
- https://www.buildwithrise.com/stories/building-with-hempcrete
- https://eurohouse.ua/en/services/building/dome-house
- https://www.biotekt.com/
- https://mymodernmet.com/skydome-round-homes/
- https://www.Earthshipglobal.com/
- https://abundance.build/
- https://www.onecommunityglobal.org/tree-house-village/
- https://www.thespruce.com/livable-tiny-house-communities-3984833
- https://www.hempitecture.com/
- https://www.onecommunityglobal.org/
- https://www.newearthliving.com.au/

Greenhouses and Gardens

- https://greenhouseinthesnow.com
- https://growingspaces.com/southwestern-united-states/
- https://www.youtube.com/watch?v=7mt8fxMfGA4
- https://towergarden.com

- https://habitathorticulture.com
- https://rareseeds.com

Books and Reading

- https://www.amazon.com/Foodscaping-Practical-Innovative-Create-Landscape/dp/1591866278/
- https://www.amazon.com/Foodscape-Revolution-Finding-Better-Beauty/dp/1943366187
- https://www.amazon.com/Edible-Landscaping-Rosalind-Creasy/dp/1578051541
- https://www.amazon.com/Handbook-Edible-Weeds-Reference-Library/dp/0849329469
- https://www.amazon.com/Second-Harvest-Helpful-Permaculture-Natural/dp/1975890957
- https://www.amazon.com/Lost-Book-Remedies-Claude-Davis/dp/1732557101
- https://www.amazon.com/Self-Sufficient-Backyard-Ron/dp/1732557160

Living Off Grid

- https://offgridliving.net/
- https://www.landsearch.com/blog/how-to-live-off-grid
- https://nogridsurvivalprojects.com

- https://topperwater.com/
- https://paleblueEarth.com
- https://luminaid.com

Metatron's Cube

You can learn more about this complex design and its many facets at https://www.youtube.com/watch?v=YhSKFVCa3V0

One of the readers of my newsletter took it upon themselves to further study Metatron's Cube and create 3-dimensional images to help each of us better understand the capabilities of this design. Here are several of the images created using his CAD design program.

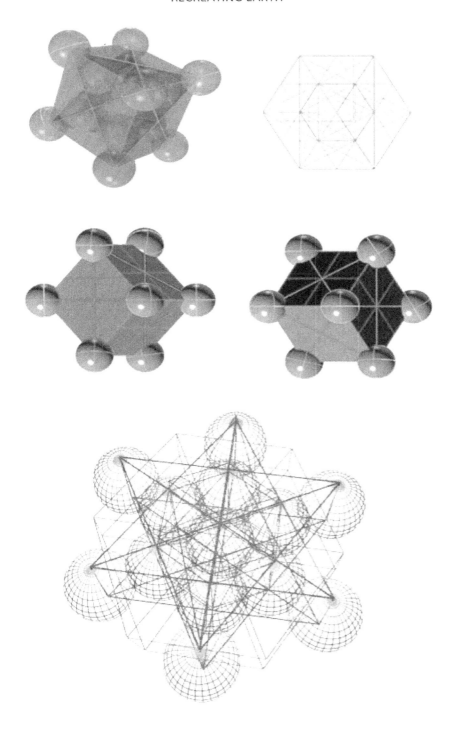

ABOUT THE AUTHOR

About the author

Victoria Reynolds is a spiritual luminary, angelic walk-in and Oracle of Freedom. Through her telepathic communications with other Ascended Masters, the Angelic Realm, Mother Earth, and Source Creator, she brings through messages for humanity from the higher realms. She also provides online and in-person classroom environments for spiritual seekers and offers one-on-one counseling services. Victoria is a multi-best-selling author, international speaker, and creator/host of *Fearless and Free TV*. You can learn more about her and her leading-edge work at *VictoriaReynolds.com*

Made in the USA
Coppell, TX
04 April 2023

15179358R00125